a DMP *production*

Accompanying Irish Music on
GUITAR
A GUIDE FOR THE CELTIC GUITARIST
by Frank Kilkelly

First produced in England 2000 by Dave Mallinson Publications
3 East View, Moorside, Cleckheaton, West Yorkshire, England BD19 6LD
Telephone +44 (0)1274 876388 *facsimile* +44 (0)1274 865208
E-mail mally@mally.com *Web* http://www.mally.com

This book and its contents are © world copyright 2000 Dave Mallinson Publications

ISBN 1 899512 57 8
A catalogue in print record for this title is available from the British Library.

The main cover picture was taken by David J Taylor and features Marion
McCarthy on uilleann pipes and Frank Kilkelly on guitar
The cover photograph of Frank was taken by Bryan Ledgard
Design and data manipulation by David J Taylor

Every reasonable effort has been made to contact copyright holders; should
anyone feel that their rights have been infringed in any way, they are urged to
contact the publishers at the above address. Should you wish to use this book
or its contents for financial gain, please contact the publishers
All rights reserved

Text set in Utopia; titling set in Impress
Pages composed in QuarkXPress

No part of Accompanying Irish Music on Guitar may be reproduced or
transmitted in any form known or as yet unknown—this includes any
electronic means such as information storage and retrieval systems—
without prior written permission from the publishers; permission is hereby
granted, however, to use extracts from this book for review purposes only
Accompanying Irish Music on Guitar is sold subject to the condition that it
shall not, by way of trade or otherwise, be lent, re-sold or otherwise
circulated without the publishers' prior consent, in any form of binding or
cover other than that in which it is published

Dave Mallinson Publications

Contents

Acknowledgements
Thanks must go to all the musicians who played on the recording: Eilish O'Connor, Mick Conneely, Teresa Heanue, Alan Kelly and Karen Ryan. Also, thanks to James Blennerhassett, Marion McCarthy, Máire O'Keeffe, Jackie Small, Jenny James and Trish Sweeney for their help along the way.

The recording

This book is designed to be used in conjunction with the compact disc recording, catalogue number DMPCD2001. Both the book and the CD are available from the publishers—whose name and address appear on the frontispiece—or through other traditional music suppliers. You may also order direct from the author via e-mail, the address being fkilkelly@hotmail.com *or by post from The Old Dispensary, Ardrahan, County Galway, Ireland.*

© 2000 Dave Mallinson Publications

About the author

Frank Kilkelly grew up in Castlebar, County Mayo and learned his craft playing in countless pub and house sessions around the west of Ireland. From 1986 to 1998 he lived in London where he played and recorded with a string of well-respected acoustic groups, including *Zumzeaux* and *The Kimbara Brothers* as well as regular work with *Luke Daniels, Brendan Power* and US dancer *Ira Bernstein*. In addition, from 1995 to 1997, he toured regularly in Europe and the USA with Irish singer *Sean Keane* and also with piano accordion player *Alan Kelly*. Equal passion for Irish traditional music and swing jazz have led to a guitar style which keeps Frank much in demand on the acoustic music scene. Since moving back to County Galway in 1998, he has been touring and recording with *Christy O'Leary, Maggie Boyle* and *Alan Kelly*, who features on the companion soundtrack to this book.

Foreword

Welcome to this guide to the accompaniment of Irish dance music on guitar.

It is designed for those who have a basic grasp of some chords and some strumming ability on the guitar. I don't assume that you know much about the structure of Irish music and so this book will also be of use if you are a competent guitarist in other styles.

The accompaniment of Irish dance music has come a long way since the first attempts in the 1920s and today there is a rich diversity of styles. Use of the guitar for accompaniment has rapidly increased since the '70s, when people like Mícheál Ó Domhnaill and Paul Brady introduced new ways of playing. However, very little has been written about this developing art and so I decided that it was time to present this book, an introduction to a handful of popular styles.

This book and companion recording give an insight into some of the many guitar styles that have been developed to accompany Irish music. By the word style, I refer to a combination of the choice of tuning, chords, right hand strumming & picking pattern, tone, etc. Several styles of accompaniment are introduced and explained in a way that is designed to help improve the developing players' analytical skills, making further exploration easier. I introduce four different tunings and several different ways of playing in each tuning. I couldn't hope to present an exhaustive range of styles and I have not attempted to create a complete directory. However, by analysing the styles I have presented, I cover all of the elements that go into making any style, thereby leaving you better equipped to both develop your own style and figure out the subtleties of any other style you may come across. For example, the factors that make up a particular strumming style are the plectrum gauge, the way the plectrum is held, whether the movement is from the wrist or the elbow—or a combination of both—the level of attack, the angle of the plectrum to the strings, the striking position along the strings—near the soundhole or the bridge—and so on. By being aware of these variables, we can take a more pro-active learning approach and the process becomes less of a hit-and-miss affair.

The recording is presented as an essential companion to the book because of the difficulty in trying to convey all of the elements of any (rhythm) guitar style solely in written form. I felt that the recording would transmit such elements as the exact accenting of some rhythms in a more comprehensible way than any amount of dots, lines and numbers would do. Also, hearing the accompaniment in place with some excellent melody players will give you a clear picture of what it is supposed to sound like. Each track appears both with and without accompaniment so you can have a go yourself when you feel ready. To help you find your way around the CD, the track numbers appear within a CD symbol where appropriate.

In your endeavours, bear in mind that it's good to be able to put technique aside when it comes to playing music (as opposed to practising). The more comfortable you are in your ability, the more you will be able to do this and put heart and soul into your playing. Whether you're playing in an informal acoustic session or performing on stage to a listening audience, as your technique becomes second nature to you, you will be better able to concentrate on everything else. It's good to take your playing seriously but when it comes to having fun with what you've learned, the less you need to worry about technique, the better. So, in the course of learning to play or improving your playing, don't forget that whatever you're learning, you're learning it so that you can forget about it when the time comes to have some fun. Good luck!

Frank Kilkelly

Introduction

So, you're planning to learn about the accompaniment of Irish music. Now you're ready to pick up the guitar and have a go at some of the accompaniment explained in the following pages. Before you start, I would like to point out that playing good rhythm guitar is not easy. It looks easy. Once you can do it, it is relatively easy. But if you haven't tried it before, it's going to feel and sound uncomfortable. That's the bad news; the good news is that it will definitely come with practice, as long as you keep listening to yourself and working on what it is you're trying to achieve. The rhythm players whose playing I enjoy have done an awful lot of playing and have developed their sense of rhythm and time to a fine degree. But please don't be put off by this. If you accept that it's going to take some time, you will enjoy the learning experience as well as the prospect of becoming a good rhythm guitarist.

How the book is structured

Section 1 of the book has some general background information about accompaniment. In section 2, I offer some guidelines to help you in your approach to studying and playing the guitar. Section 3 is the main section, which was created in tandem with the accompanying soundtrack. In it I take a close look at a number of different ways of approaching accompaniment. On the soundtrack there are 14 sets of popular session tunes, with accompaniment using various right hand styles and four different tunings.

The corresponding section in the book has notes on the style used, as well as chord windows for every chord shape used and a chord chart to show you when to play each chord.

Now, the intention is not to teach you the accompaniment for 20 or so tunes but to impart a repertoire of chords, phrases, rhythmic tricks and so on. Once you can play them, they can be applied to many different tunes. If you like, think of this book as a starter pack for a language course and after you've got what you can from it, you can build on this base with your own ideas plus ones you might pick up from other sources. Alternatively, this book may help to expand an already proficient accompaniment repertoire. To take different levels of ability into account, I accompanied many of the tunes on the recording very simply on the first time round and the variations appear on the second time round the tune.

Throughout the book I have references to the appendix, which offers more technical explanations of some areas. Refer to it if you feel so inclined but it's not essential learning; perhaps you can refer to it at some other time than when you have the guitar on your lap.

How to use this book

I suggest you approach the book in the following way:

1 Take an hour or so to read through the introductory chapters so you get a clear idea of the purpose of the book.

2 Read closely the section on notation used in the book, until you become fluent at reading the chord charts and windows. Having selected a track from the recording that appeals to you, read the notes on the accompaniment for that set of tunes and all of the background information relating to the style being used.

3 Next, break the learning task into its component parts:

(a) Learn to play all of the chords used in the set of tunes you've chosen, until you can finger them instantly. Should you need it, left hand fingering for the chords is shown in the chord directory in the appendix.

(b) Learn to play the chords in progressions. I suggest you use the learning exercise in section 2. Don't think about the rhythm just yet, if it's new to you. If the chords are changing too fast on the recording for you to play along, you should use a metronome to learn the chord progressions at a slower but regular pace. Once you've built up speed with chord changing, figure out the best way to play the rhythm on the track using a combination of *my* description of the right hand style, *your* ears and *your* intuition.

(c) Try it with the unaccompanied version of the track you've been working on.

The companion recording

The recording has 40 tracks in all. On each of tracks 1 to 14 there are two tunes played with accompaniment. The guitar is panned to the right. If you want to hear more of the guitar, turn your balance control to the right or listen on headphones.

15 to 26 are the DADGAD examples illustrated in Section 3·5.

Then, on tracks 27 to 40, the same tunes as on tracks 1 to 14 appear without accompaniment. So, track 27 is the same as track 1, without the accompaniment and so on. Tracks 15 to 26 has the examples given in section 3·5 on DADGAD.

The tunes are played by some of the finest musicians playing Irish music today and include Mick Conneely and Karen Ryan on fiddles, tracks 1, 2 and 9, Mick playing solo on track 11, Teresa Heanue on fiddle, tracks 5 and 13, Alan Kelly on piano accordion, tracks 3, 4, 6, 7, 10 and 12 and Eilish O'Connor on fiddle, tracks 8 and 14.

To summarise

This book offers an introduction to accompanying tunes in four different tunings, using several different right hand approaches. A repertoire of chords is included, along with suggestions about strumming/picking styles suitable for each tuning. The idea is that you learn the accompaniment as played on the track. This will increase your chord vocabulary and will help you with right hand techniques.

© 2000 Dave Mallinson Publications

Section 1

1·0 THE DEVELOPING ART OF ACCOMPANIMENT

1·1 The emergence of the guitar in the accompaniment of Irish music

Today's repertoire of reels, jigs and hornpipes dates back to the seventeenth century. The only evidence of Irish music before that time lies in the harping tradition. For most of its life, the music has been played on melody instruments such as fiddle and uilleann pipes without any accompaniment other than the percussive addition of bodhrán, bones, spoons or the sounds of dancing feet.

The first recordings of Irish music with chordal accompaniment (usually on piano) were the 78 rpm records made in America in the early 1900s by musicians such as Michael Coleman and James Morrison. A bigger sound was necessary for playing to large numbers of people and as traditional music was very popular with Irish emigrants in the US at the time, the piano was added to fill out the sound. Presumably also, it was felt by recording companies that the accompaniment was an improvement which gave the music a wider appeal and at the time it probably did.

Because accompanying Irish music was new, styles of accompaniment were borrowed from other genres of music and it is evident from many of these early recordings that the accompanists were depending heavily on their ears, rather than their knowledge of the tunes. Judging from the choice of chords and the style of playing on some of the early recordings, it is obvious that the accompanists, (or 'backers' as they are called) would have been more comfortable playing barrelhouse, boogie-woogie or stride piano!

Although some recordings featured guitar backing, the piano was more popular and when the recordings were imported and released in Ireland, the piano style of accompaniment was taken up and widely used in céilí bands right up to the sixties.

By this time however, the guitar was gaining world-wide popularity, assisted in the folk world by people like The Clancys, Bob Dylan and Martin Carthy. Its inevitable introduction to Irish music came as a mixed blessing. While it offered a portable alternative to the piano, with an acoustic volume and tone which was more suited to the other instruments, it sometimes attracted players who were less than competent (or interested in becoming so). These players could now join in the session with barely any knowledge of the music. Many of these players were first and foremost ballad singers, who used the guitar to accompany their songs, often with limited ability. As a result, the guitar developed a poor reputation amongst tune players and in fact it was banned from all sessions and events organised by Comhaltas Ceoltóirí Éireann, the organisation set up in 1951 to promote Irish music and dance. I was myself witness to this when a performance organised by CCÉ was once halted while I was removed from the stage! Thankfully, the revival of Irish music from the late '60s onwards was strong enough to wade through opposing conservative forces and the music has developed to include many new instruments being used in new ways, among them the guitar.

A definition of accompaniment

For the most part, accompaniment of Irish music (other than on percussion) is harmonically sympathetic, polyphonic rhythmic embellishment which is played on either a strummed string instrument such as guitar or bouzouki, or a keyed string instrument such as piano or (rarely) harpsichord. The accompaniment can add a driving rhythm to carry the tune along, or enhance a mood being suggested by the tune. Also, dynamic variations within each set of tunes are more pronounced as a good accompanist can vary the mood more effectively from tune to tune.

Personally, the sort of accompaniment that appeals to me is that which locks in with the melody player(s), embellishing the nuances and flavour of the tune with rhythmic and chordal variations but at the same time not getting in the way of the tune, in other words, being unobtrusive to the listener. Of course, there are players who don't satisfy these criteria but whose playing I love. In general, however, the above are the guidelines I use for my own playing.

Photo: Tony C Kearns

Session in Conway's bar, Mullagh, County Clare
Seán Fitzpatrick (guitar), Seamus MacMahon (fiddle) and Dermot Lernihan (accordeon)

© 2000 Dave Mallinson Publications

1·2 Profiles of leading players

*h*ere, in alphabetical order, I list my favourite accompanists plus, more importantly, players who I personally think have made or are making a significant contribution to the broadening of accompaniment styles.

Randal Bays

Randal lives in Seattle, Oregon and is also a fine fiddler. His guitar playing has been greatly influenced by his friend Mícheál Ó Domhnaill, who lived in Portland for many years. I first heard the subtle playing of Randal on fiddler Martin Hayes' first two albums. Martin's sensitive fiddle style calls for an empathetic and soft accompaniment style, which is played in DADGAD.

Ed Boyd

Ed's playing came to light in the three flute band, *Flook!* His style has a light, energetic feel and he uses some unusual rhythms in his playing. He uses mostly DADGAD but occasionally standard tuning.

Paul Brady

From his work with the *Johnstons*, through *Planxty* and a solo career, Paul Brady has been a central figure in the revival and development of traditional Irish music. He played as accompanist on a handful of recordings made by notable fiddle players, particularly on the *Shanachie* label. He plays mostly in standard tuning with the occasional excursion into dropped D and his style is characterised by a crisp percussive tone, with great attack. He also makes good use of rhythmic variations, which punctuate his aggressive, driving style on up-tempo sets of tunes.

Dennis Cahill

Dennis has arrived on the international folk scene in recent years as playing partner to Martin Hayes. His background is very varied. Having studied classical guitar he played on the Chicago live music circuit for years in more genres than most. He uses standard tuning and his accompaniment of Martin's fiddle playing is harmonically rich and full of space. His playing breaks the mould of twenty or more years and is well worth a listen.

Ian Carr

He is best known for his playing with Northumbrian piper and fiddler Kathryn Tickell and piano accordion player Karen Tweed. He has a style all of his own, in which he breaks the boundaries created by the developing styles of accompaniment. With a strong emphasis on arrangements, a lot happens in the course of a set of tunes when Ian's playing. He is one of the most original accompanists that I've come across and I recommend a listen, to hear a totally fresh approach.

Steve Cooney

Since his arrival in Ireland from Australia around the late 1970s, Steve has had a major impact on the accompaniment of Irish music, on nylon-strung guitar as well as on bass guitar. In particular, his style of backing Kerry slides and polkas is well worth checking out. He has worked with many leading Irish musicians, notably Liam O'Flynn and Donal Lunny. His work appears on almost a hundred recordings, displaying a huge versatility in styles, all with a distinct, original flavour.

John Doyle

Based in the east coast American music scene, John has a powerful rhythmic approach to accompaniment. He combines a repertoire of full-bodied chords with a tireless strumming arm to provide a steady rhythm for the melody players. He tunes his guitar to dropped D and is the rhythmic centre of leading Irish/US group *Solas*.

Donogh Hennessey

Donogh established his style and reputation with Sharon Shannon's band and more recently as a member of *Lunasa*. A superb rhythm player, he tunes to DADGBD (double dropped D) and his careful choices of chord sequences are worth noting in the accompaniment he plays. He works closely with the bass player (Trevor Hutchinson) and together they make a tight sound, which offers a rock-solid underpinning for the melody players. Listen to this teamwork on any of the listed albums.

Peerie Willie Johnson

Willie and his friend, pianist Ronnie Cooper, were largely responsible for a major development in the accompaniment of Scottish and particularly Shetland music. Willie adapted the swing jazz rhythm guitar style to accompany dance tunes. The style is characterised by a 'boom-chuck' rhythm where the first and third beats in the bar are primarily bass notes ('boom') and the second and fourth play the rest of the chord ('chuck'), which is damped.

Mark Kelly

Mark has been the guitarist with *Altan* since their formation in 1982 and his playing has been a major part of the development of the sound of the band. On early recordings he was tuned to DADF♯AD but more recently he has been using DADGAD, DGDGBD, dropped D (DADGBE) and double dropped D (DADGBD).

Arty McGlynn

Since the release of his solo album in 1980 Arty has become one the most sought-after accompanists on the traditional music scene today and has played on countless folk albums in Ireland. In accompanying, his style is first and foremost rhythmic. He uses primarily dropped D tuning and in his playing you can hear a percussive, crispy top end, as well as a beefy bass sound.

Mícheál Ó Domhnaill

The Bothy Band was possibly the most innovative traditional band to ever come out of Ireland and Mícheál was the rhythmic centre, playing guitar mainly tuned to DADGAD but occasionally using standard tuning. He developed a whole new style, playing chunky, solid chords. He is worth listening to as he was one of the earliest innovators in the genre and his playing continues to have an impact on many players (directly or indirectly), twenty years on.

Dáithí Sproule

Dáithí has been the favourite choice of many excellent traditional melody players in America for a long time. He uses DADGAD and occasionally standard tuning. He shares the guitar role in *Altan* with Mark Kelly and in addition plays in a trio called *Trian* with Liz Carroll and Billy McComisky.

These players have all had a different impact on the development of styles and this is essentially a subjective collection. By giving a little information on these players, the intention is that you will hopefully like the sound of some of these guitarists and check them out further yourself. The discography for these is included in the appendix.

© 2000 Dave Mallinson Publications

When you're listening to Irish music, try to identify the different keys, time signatures and structures of the tunes. You'll find, for example, many tunes in the key of D, in $\frac{4}{4}$, (reel or hornpipe time), with two parts, each eight bars long and each played twice, giving a structure, A-A-B-B. As a typical example, have a look at the chords for *Pigeon on the gate* as shown in *Figure 1* below. It may help to listen to this tune on the CD at the same time.

A working knowledge of this information gives vital clues to what's coming next if you're not familiar with the tune. If you know the tune, a knowledge of the structure gives more freedom to play interesting variations on each repeat of the tune. By developing both your harmonic sense and your chord repertoire, you will increase your chances of hitting the right chord.

1·3 Accompanying tunes effectively

There are three rules: listen, listen and listen!

Listen to other accompanists

Among guitarists, there is a wide variety of styles, with explorations into harmony, rhythm and alternative tunings providing new ways to accompany Irish music. The best advice I can give is to cultivate your taste in accompaniment by listening to recordings and performances of different players. Recordings are sometimes of limited use, depending on the volume of the guitar in the mix. However, there are many albums by fine melody players, with clearly audible accompaniment. (See the discography in the appendix for suggestions).

In a live situation you get a better chance to figure out what's going on in the rhythm department, as you can see what both hands are doing. Listen carefully for rhythms, as in my opinion that's the single most important factor in good accompaniment. Good sense of time is really important and the tempo of the accompaniment should lock in with the melody players. It should support it, without speeding up or slowing down.

When playing, listen to the tune

Here are a few points that may help you:

1 It is not possible to back a tune you don't know. There seems to be a popular misconception that since the guitarist is not playing the melody of the tune, he or she does not have to know the tune in order to add accompaniment. This is almost totally untrue and has led in part to the tarnished reputation of guitarists in the session scene, both in Ireland and overseas. However, it has to be said that a well-accomplished accompanist can make some intelligent guesses with an unfamiliar tune and if there are no unpredictable shifts, the result can be very presentable. For the most part, each tune should be regarded as a song, with a chord structure that is in most places rigid and in some places flexible, with room for a few alternative chords. If you're playing in a session and a tune starts that you're not familiar with, use the first time round the tune to listen and figure out the key, some pivotal chords, (like the first chord for each part), the number of parts, etc. *As a general rule I will only join in if I think I can add something to the music.* If the tune is unusual and difficult to follow, the best thing to do is probably to listen and get to know the tune, though you may want to join in.

2 Most keys have a small repertoire of chords, which, once you know them, are pretty safe to try. For example in Em, the judicious use of D, Bm, G

and C will get you through most tunes. In major keys, careful use of the 3-chord trick often works. Remember, keep it simple, you don't have to change chords for the sake of it! In some of the tunes on the recording, I demonstrate how although you can get through a tune comfortably on 3 chords, you can also make it a lot more colourful by adding extra chords. For example, have a listen to *The mist-covered mountain* on Track 1.

3 You should be aware of where the rhythmic emphases are in a tune. They define the pulse and part of the accompanist's role is to pin down the pulse. In jigs (which have six beats in each bar) the emphasis is generally on the first and (to a lesser degree) the fourth beats, whereas reels (which have four beats per bar) generally have the emphasis on the first and third beats, again with a stronger beat on the first measure.

4 Get to know the tunes. I found that when I learnt to play the tunes, I was able to accompany them more accurately. If you have the time and the inclination, why not pick up a mandolin or tenor banjo and learn to play some of the melodies? It will help you to get inside the tunes and it will also help your plectrum control, which will in turn help your guitar playing! (Incidentally, it's much easier to learn melodies on instruments tuned like a fiddle, i.e. GDAE, which is why I suggest tenor banjo or mandolin, rather than guitar.)

Listen to your own playing

Listen as you play and listen to recordings of yourself. As you play, listen to the rhythm you're playing, the chords you're using, the relative volume of yourself to the other players, etc. There is a lot to be learned if we constantly re-assess our playing, with a view to how it can be improved. Listening to recordings of ourselves can be alarming, because, removed from the adrenaline of actually playing and the fun (or drunkenness) of the session, it may not sound quite like we thought it did! However, generally, recordings don't lie, (although the tone may suffer) so they give accurate feedback on your playing. Remember, look for qualities you like about your playing as well as areas that need some work so that you get positive encouragement as well as constructive criticism, albeit from yourself. Beware of a tendency to discard some good things you're doing because on the whole you're disappointed with how it sounds. Perhaps the rhythm doesn't sound quite right because you're using a plectrum of the wrong gauge, for example.

Figure 1: second time through *Pigeon on the gate*

A3	Em		Em	A7	D	G	D/F♯	Bm	Em		Em	A7	D	G	Bm	Em
A4	Em		Em	A7	D	G	D/F♯	Bm	Em		Em	A7	D	G	Bm	Em
B3	Em		Em	A7	D		D/F♯		Em		Em	G	D/F♯	G	Bm	Em
B4	Em		Em	A7	D		Bm		Em		Em	A7	D	G	Bm	Em

© 2000 Dave Mallinson Publications

Section 2

2·0 Getting Started

2·1 Guide to choosing equipment

In this section, I take a look at the tools for the job, which is an area often neglected by people who use their instruments to make a living, as well as by those who play for fun.

Traditional backing can be played on almost any guitar. Although the majority of players tend to use steel-strung models, there is a recent trend towards nylon-strung guitars. What is more important is the condition of the instrument. My guitar was transformed after its first trip to a professional guitar technician. I took my guitar along with a minor complaint of a buzz on one fret and the technician pointed out several little adjustments to the nut, saddle, neck and frets that in the end made a huge improvement to the feel and sound of the guitar. In the south of England, I highly recommend *Bill Puplett Guitars* for a professional set-up. His number is 0208 954 1965.

Even new guitars are not always set up as well as they might; be aware of this in your search for a guitar. I've had some inexpensive guitars sound and play very well because they have been set up properly for the way I play. Of course, preferences vary in terms of set-up; for example, gentle players prefer a lower action to more heavy-handed players. Also, if you're mostly playing using amplification, you may find that because you don't need to generate a high level of acoustic volume, you can develop styles using low action and a more subtle approach.

Buying a guitar

The most common steel-strung acoustic guitar design is known as a *dreadnought*. Most major manufacturers make a dreadnought size in their range. They fall into two main categories: laminated top and solid top. This means what it says; the top on the solid is made from a single piece of wood (although sometimes in two halves) whereas a laminated top is made of several thin layers of wood glued together like plywood. Laminated tops are less expensive, mass-produced instruments and they vary in quality from poor to not bad at all. Solid top guitars are coming down in price all the time and although they also vary enormously in quality, on average they are far better instruments, with more potential for ageing into even better sounding instruments.

Making a purchase is always a difficult business, especially if you don't know exactly what you want. Trying out guitars in shops can be less than satisfying for many reasons. If possible, get a sale or return deal so that you can have some time to play it in your home. I recommend you spend only as much as your ears demand, moving to a better instrument only when your ears tire of the shortcomings of your current guitar. Don't buy a very expensive instrument if your ears can't tell the difference between it and a mid-range model even if you can afford it, as you'll be missing a step in the training of your ears to the nuances of tone.

Strings

There's a huge variety of strings specifically designed for acoustic steel-string guitar. They vary in gauge and material and different brands have inherently different tension, though not stated on the pack. Try out different brands, materials and gauges and cultivate your taste based on how they feel and sound, how long they last before losing their brightness and how much they cost. A popular choice in general is phosphor-bronze light gauge, with a first of ·012" and a sixth of ·053". Some suppliers have started packaging sets suitable for DADGAD with heavier first, second and sixth to compensate for the slightly lower tension. The life of strings on your guitar will depend on how much you play and how much your hands sweat as you play. Some players use the same strings for weeks and others change their strings before every gig.

Plectrums/picks

These are also available in an endless variety of gauges, materials, finishes and colours. I suggest you buy a range of different types and vary the level and angle of attack, position along the strings, etc, to find a sound and feel that suits you. The plectrum plays a large part in the tone you get from the instrument. Having one that feels right will help your rhythm playing to become smoother. If you have sweaty hands you may like the type that have a rough surface on the part you hold. You could drill a hole through the centre of the plectrum to give you a better grip. It's worth staying with well-known and well-stocked brands in case you settle on one kind only to find that a replacement cannot be had. The way you hold the pick is a factor to consider and you should check out the way that different players hold theirs. I hold mine as shown in *Figure 2.*

Figure 2: How to hold the plectrum

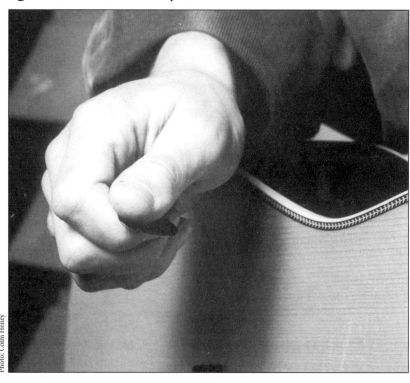

Photo: Colm Henry

© 2000 Dave Mallinson Publications

Capos

There is a wide range of capos on the market and many guitarists seem to be in an endless search for the perfect one. There is a compromise between mobility (up and down the neck) and grip. For accompanying Irish music, especially in open tunings, you need both. Ideally, a capo should grip enough that the strings ring clear but not so tight that the strings are squeezed in to the neck and out of tune. This criterion is more difficult to achieve with some capos because the neck is thicker near the body; the correct tension in one position is thus too tight in another. Adjustable capos are one way around this but then moving the capo along the neck becomes a big affair.

A good quality elastic capo is probably the best option; if you use it a lot, be prepared to replace it fairly regularly. I currently use a very successful self-adjusting capo called *QuickDraw*, made by a small company in America. It is made of steel and coated in Teflon so it's very easy to move up and down the neck. They are available in the US directly from the manufacturers and for customers in Europe I carry a small stock myself. Quickdraw capos can be accessed by e-mail at qkdraw@nh.ultranet.com or obtained directly from me at Ardrahan, County Galway, Ireland.

Amplification

Thankfully, the world of amplifying acoustic guitars has made huge progress in the last twenty years or so. Many acoustic guitars with factory installed pick-up systems have a decent sound. However, if you want to go about customising your own pick-up system, the first thing I should do is wish you luck, because it can be very much a hit and miss affair, depending on how particular you are. What sounds really good in one guitar might not work so well for another. However, there is a wide range of different systems available, from simple transducer type pick-ups that

are mounted under the saddle (the bit that the strings rest on at the bridge), to multiple source systems that take signals from a few places and blend them together to give a more accurate acoustic sound. Pickups can be supplemented by microphones (either fitted internally or used externally on a stand), to give a more 'wooden' sound, as many pick-ups can sound rather harsh and sibilant on their own.

Taking cost, quality and technical complexity into account, the most satisfactory set-up that I've come across has been a transducer pickup fitted at the bridge and an internal microphone fitted somewhere near the soundhole, wired into a stereo socket at the endpin jack. A stereo lead from the guitar to a splitter box enables you to split the signals and blend a mix of the microphone and the pickup, as well changing the equalisation (treble and bass) of either signal.

Hipshot tuners & Keith pegs

The *Hipshot* tuner is a mechanism that is fitted in place of the peg for the sixth string. It incorporates a replacement peg and also has a flip lever to drop the string down a tone to D. In my experience, they work well and make it possible to change between standard tuning and Dropped D while playing. *Keith* banjo pegs do the same job but work in a different way. They can be used to replace any peg and they look like banjo pegs with two little thumbscrews on the side. These are used to set upper and lower limits of travel. So, for example, you tune the string to E and tighten the high limit screw. Then you tune the string to D and you tighten the low limit screw. The peg is then locked so that it will go no further down than D and no further up than E.

I have them fitted on the first and second strings so that, in conjunction with the Hipshot tuner, I can change very quickly and accurately between any tunings I use. You may find that grating some pencil lead into the string slots in the nut will help the string to slide up and down more smoothly and hence remain more in tune.

EQ boxes

As many acoustic musicians use amplification nowadays, I consider it a tremendous advantage to be familiar with the basics of sound engineering. There are many good, accessible books on the subject and I suggest you have a good read if you want to be able to converse comfortably with sound engineers, the people who are responsible for presenting *your* sound to *your* audience.

However, there is one very useful area that I feel compelled to mention here. EQ is short for *equalisation*, which is the process of shaping sound while on its journey from the pickup/microphone to the loudspeaker. An EQ box is a metal box that has two sockets; your guitar plugs into one and the other is connected to the PA or amplifier. It has the means of cutting or boosting a range of different frequencies, from low to high. It may have sliding controls or knobs. A good EQ unit can be very effective in sorting out a problem in the sound source or it can be used to make a good signal even better. Some floor boxes have a footswitch so that you can switch the EQ on and off while playing; perhaps you prefer a different sound for taking a solo, for example.

Pickups

The best advice I can give is to approach players whose sound you like and ask them what pick-up system they use; also, seek the advice of an expert, who should recommend the most suitable set-up for your guitar.

Photo: Tony C Kearns

Steve Cooney

© 2000 Dave Mallinson Publications

2·2 Developing a practice routine

*I*f you intend to progress as a guitarist, it's worth taking a long-term learning approach. Many professionals continue to practice all their lives in order to keep an edge to their playing and because you never know everything—there's always something new to learn.

Now although some people are happy slouched on a sofa doodling away on the guitar with the television on, it's not really an efficient, organised or comfortable way to approach practice. I recommend you take the following steps to getting organised as a guitar student.

1 Dedicate an area of your home to practising. It doesn't have to be solely for practice, simply a space where you have everything you need to hand. It only needs to be a corner of a room, with a small table, for a tape recorder or compact disc player, room for your books, some paper, pens and pencils, a metronome, enough light to be able to see and any other learning aids you use. If you get organised in this way, you'll find fewer excuses to avoid the practice that everybody finds difficult.

2 Make some regular time available for practice. Examine your typical day and see where you can claw back a regular amount of time every day, or a few times a week. Depending on your routine, this may be early in the morning, or early in the evening. Don't expect much of yourself late at night, as concentration is hardest then. Try not to make unrealistic plans, because if you can't meet them, you may become disillusioned and give up. It's better to decide on 20 minutes every day than plan to do an hour and fail to put the time in. Also, regular small intervals are better than irregular long sessions. Once you've decided that come hell or high water, you're going to spend a certain regular amount of time with the guitar, the rest is relatively easy. Whether you do this or not will depend on how much you really want to learn or improve.

3 OK, you've made the time slots in your weekly diary, now what? I suggest you use the first few sessions to devise a plan for yourself. Decide what it is you want to learn and work backwards. For example, with folk tune accompaniment, there is a certain amount of basic chord theory that will help increase your understanding of what's going on and there's also a physical skill to be developed. Plan an amount of time to be spent in each session on each of these aspects so that neither is neglected. You may find the practical side easier, in which case you should possibly do the non-playing part first, to keep the dessert for later, as it were! In general, the brain can only take in a certain amount of new information at any time, whereas the development of physical motor skills calls for longer sessions—a bit like jogging. Of course, there may be periods when you are focussed on one small area and other stuff is being neglected; something of interest may draw you in and you may find yourself engrossed totally in, say, fingerstyle arrangements of Irish tunes in some new tuning. That's fine, as long as you're aware that you're on a diversion from the planned route and you re-route your future plans accordingly.

4 It's a good idea to devise some ways to measure your progress. As adults, we often forget that it took us years (literally) of comprehensive practice and study to learn to read and write. It's unrealistic to expect to acquire a skill just as complex in a much shorter time, with any less effort. As a ten-year-old guitar pupil, I remember finding a chord of E all by my little self and I got weeks of gratification out of it. Unfortunately, as we grow older, we know too much about the bigger picture and we have our sights set on where we want to be, rather than where we are right now. This is probably the biggest psychological obstacle to learning anything, as adults. So, I have found it very useful to devise ways of measuring progress; at the end of a certain period, you can look back and say, "I can do something now that I couldn't do then."

(a) Make a practice progress chart. Draw a grid chart, with the days of the week on the vertical axis and the metronome speed on the other. Create some exercises from any area of interest, say, a sequence of chords, a picking pattern, anything. Start at a speed at which you're comfortable and spend two or three minutes on each exercise. Use a kitchen timer to time the minutes so that you stick rigidly to the plan. Once you can play at a certain speed, put a tick in the appropriate box, move up a notch on the metronome and start again. You'll be surprised at how quickly you build up a facility this way. The other advantage of using a metronome is that it regulates the body's internal rhythm machine and turns us into good timekeepers. No, it's nothing to do with being late for work, it's about being able to play in time, without (unconsciously) speeding up or slowing down.

(b) Try this test of your ability to stay in time. Set your metronome to a slow click, play along with it, playing anything, from a single note on one string to a rhythm pattern. See how long you can remain in time with the click. Some people have no problem with this and others find it very difficult. If you've never done this before and find it easy to remain in time with the click, you have a good inherent sense of time. If you strayed within about 20 seconds you need to spend time playing along with a metronome to build up your internal rhythm.

(c) Record yourself playing. Make the recording as good as you can and listen to it with constructively critical ears. If you are analytical, you should be able to figure out exactly what is needed to improve the quality of what you're hearing. For example, perhaps it's good for the most part but it slows down (or speeds up) when it gets to a difficult bit; (remedy; do some concentrated practice on that bit). Alternatively, you may decide that your strumming is not very smooth; (remedy; more concentrated strumming practice [with metronome], experiment with different picks, angles of strike, etc)

The beauty of the guitar is that there are so many facets to it. If you're bored practising one element of interest, you can do something else. For example, if you've had enough of scales, or learning new chords, you can put on a recording to play along with and have some fun, while improving an element of your playing as well.

It has to be said that the number one way to become more proficient at right hand techniques such as strumming is to do it as much as possible. Many right hand techniques are deceptive, in that they appear fairly simple, until you try them. Strumming and picking technique is difficult to get across in written form but if you pay close attention to the suggestions I have made throughout the book and use your ears and your intuition, you should progress quickly. With chords, perseverance may be necessary, as new positions for your fingerboard hand can be very tiring at first. Just remember that the first chords you learnt felt awkward until your hand got to know them well.

Tip: if you're practising scales or a series of chord changes, always use a metronome

© 2000 Dave Mallinson Publications

2·3 Notation used in this book

Tablature

In tablature, the six horizontal lines represent the six strings, with the first string on top and the sixth on the bottom. The numbers refer to fret numbers on the given string. 0 refers to an open string. The vertical lines mark out the bars in this example, marking four beats between each line, as in standard music notation. In this book, many of the right hand patterns are played with the left hand held in one position (like a chord) for that section of music and where this is the case, the chord windows appear over the relevant section.

Figure 3: Sample tablature

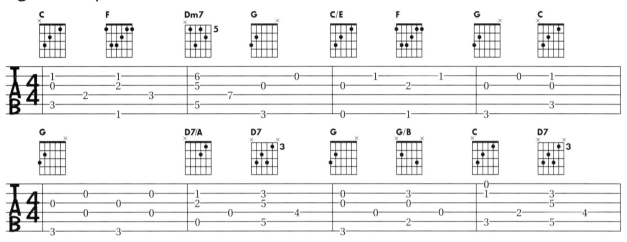

Chord diagrams (chord windows)

Chord diagrams show where the fingers go on the fretboard. Two examples are shown in *Figure 4.* The horizontal lines refer to the frets and the vertical lines refer to the strings, with the lowest string (sixth) on the left. A heavy line on the top of the diagram refers to either the nut (the white strip which the strings ride over at the peghead end of the neck) or the capo. If the heavy line is present, the window refers to frets 1 to 4 from the nut or the capo. Otherwise, the number at the right of the diagram refers to a fret number. Likewise, this refers to the number of frets from either the nut or the capo, depending upon whether a capo is in use or not.

X indicates a string that should be muted or not played.

Figure 4: Sample chords

Chord charts

These are fairly straightforward and are written out in eight bar lines, which is generally one part of a tune. This means that in a standard tune four lines of chords will make up one time around the tune, in a standard A-A-B-B form. For ease of reference, each part is labelled A1 through A4 and B1 through B4. Where I have put a number after a chord, refer to the chord windows and you'll find there is more than one version of this chord. Play the numbered one. When there is more than one chord per bar, split the time for each chord equally in the bar, unless otherwise indicated by markers. For example, in a bar of $\frac{4}{4}$, if you have [Bm / / A], you play Bm for three beats and A for the fourth.

Lower case letters refer to bass notes, which are usually played on the sixth or fifth string. Shaded sections of the chart means that there is a reference to this somewhere in the text.

The capo and written chords

Now, the capo is a great invention in practice but when it comes to writing down chords, it can cause great confusion. This is because when using a capo, any chord will change its name, i.e. it will be a different chord and its new name depends on where the capo is placed. For example if you play a D chord with the capo on the second fret, it's an E chord. The same chord played with the capo on the third fret is an F chord and so on.

I want to clear up any possible misunderstanding that may develop because of this. If a capo has been used on the recording, I have stated so clearly in the comments relating to that track. In some cases, a change of capo position happens between the first and second tune on the same track and this is made clear also.

Now, please note that the chords in the charts are written as if there was no capo in use. The idea is that you can slide your capo to the stated position and read the chords as if you were not using a capo. With the chord windows, fret numbers refer to either the number of frets from the nut, or from the capo, if one is in use.

© 2000 Dave Mallinson Publications

Section 3

3·0 GUIDE TO TUNINGS AND ACCOMPANIMENT STYLES

In this section, I take a look at the structure of some popular types of tunes. Next, I have devised some definitions of right-hand styles in order to classify them in some way. In my own experience, certain right-hand approaches suit some tunings better than others and some suit some types of tunes better than others and so on. Of course, you should experiment freely to find what works best for you.

3·1 The structure of Irish tunes

The repertoire of Irish music is composed mainly of reels, jigs and hornpipes, with variations such as polkas, slides, slip jigs, single jigs and less common forms such as marches, barn dances and mazurkas. This book deals only with reels, jigs and hornpipes but it is useful to know the form of these other kinds of tunes, so I recommend you read one of the many good books available on the subject.

Jigs

§ is the time signature here, which means there are six beats in each bar, each with a one eighth measure. A standard jig has two parts, which we will call an A part and a B part. (The B part is sometimes called the high part or the *turn*).

The parts are the same length, usually eight bars. The parts are usually played twice, with a different ending for each time.

When listening to a tune, the phrase *bopity-bopity* may help you to ascertain if it's a jig, as it has the same rhythmic feel as a § rhythm. Although most jigs have two parts some have three, four or more. For example, see **Doctor O'Neill,** (page 30) which has five parts, each played twice.

Reels

Reels have a time signature of ⁴⁄₄, which means that there are four beats in each bar and each beat is a quarter measure. As with jigs, reels generally have two parts, of eight bars in length. Each part is played twice, with a different ending (i.e. the last bar or two of each part will be slightly different). However, some reels do not follow this pattern. Some have parts that are only four bars long and some reels have more than two parts.

When listening to a tune, the phrase *taca-taca* may help you figure out if it's a reel, as it has the same rhythmic feel as a ⁴⁄₄ rhythm. Hornpipes have the same structure, although the phrasing of the melody and the tempo are quite different.

On the soundtrack I used recording technology to disguise the changes in capo position. When playing live, I would stop in the last bar of a tune, move the capo to the next position and be ready to play for the first beat of the new tune. With practice and a good sliding capo, you will become quicker and more accurate at this.

3·2 Strumming and picking patterns

1 Bass-strum

Listen to **Pigeon on the gate** & **The Shaskeen reel.** This is a style that will be recognisable to you if you've played other styles of folk guitar, as it uses chords in standard tuning and a strumming style you may already know. A bass note is played on the first and third beats and the rest of the chord on the second and fourth beats (in a reel). The bass note played would be either the root of the chord or part of a run to the next chord. Variety and dynamics can be added by right hand rhythmic variations at appropriate places in the tune to punctuate or accentuate the melody.

2 Shetland swing

Listen to **Flogging reel** & **The whistling postman.** This style could also be referred to as *Texas swing,* depending on the kind of tunes being played. Commonly known as the *boom-chuck* style, it fits very well with reels, which are the mainstay of Shetland fiddle music. The rhythm is played as constant downbeats with an occasional punctuation on the offbeat (as an up-stroke) perhaps every eight bars. This style borrows heavily from the tradition of gypsy jazz popularised by Django Reinhardt and Stephane Grappelli in the 1930s and, as mentioned earlier, was adapted for use with Shetland fiddle tunes by Peerie Willie Johnson.

With the chords for the tunes accompanied in this style, it may be worth your while using the learning exercise in section 2·2. Although this style is similar in some ways to the bass-strum style, there are a few distinguishing traits. Firstly, damping is used, mainly on the second and fourth beats (the 'chuck'), to create a 'chopped' feel. To shorten the beat, you can either release the grip on the left hand just after the chord has been struck, damp the strings with the heel of the right hand or you can do both.

Secondly, 'closed' or mobile chord shapes are used, i.e. ones without open strings, as these add to the effect of the damping. Once you've learnt a handful of chord shapes you can use them to play in almost any key.

When playing in this style, try to avoid strumming the first and second strings, as practically all of the chords have all the necessary 'colour' notes in the bottom four strings. Also, playing just four strings adds to the feel of the rhythm for this style. So, when you get to the chord diagrams for the tunes played in this style you'll see that sometimes I've included fingerings for the first and second strings and others have been neglected; they're not important. Some have been included because the chord is easiest played in a barré shape, so although you finger the string with the left hand, you don't hit the string with the plectrum.

There are not many recordings of tunes accompanied in what I call the Shetland swing style. I would recommend having a look at any books on Gypsy jazz or Hot Club style jazz if you want to broaden your repertoire of swing chord shapes.

© 2000 Dave Mallinson Publications

3 Steady strum

This is basically a regular repeating down-up strum pattern, either covering all strings or just playing the bottom four (or five) strings. I present a few versions of this style, by varying the stroke pattern and the beats on which rhythmic emphases are placed. In each of the patterns, when changing chords, I sometimes place emphasis on the bass note of the new chord; this is achieved by a slightly heavier downbeat on the appropriate bass string. (Listen to *My love is in America*).

In some jigs, I skip the second beat, creating pattern a like this: ↓ — ↓ ↓ ↑ ↓ . By missing this second beat, the first beat is allowed to ring out a bit longer. If a new chord is not played in the bar, I tend to play each beat with equal emphasis and play an upstroke on the second beat. (Listen to *John Brady's* & *Hexham races* or *My darling asleep* & *Boys of the town*).

When strumming, depending on the tuning, I sometimes use damping with the heel of the right hand. Damping by itself muffles the note but used in conjunction with a heavy strike will create a beefy bass sound, so it's useful if you want to emphasise a bass note. To damp a string or strings, hit the strings with the plectrum and at the same time hit the strings nearer to the bridge with the heel of your right hand. (Listen to *Jerry's beaver hat* or *Fred Finn's*). To get a full sound, the movement should be from the elbow, so that the weight of your forearm is in the rhythm. Like every suggestion in this book, experiment to find what works for you. You may find it helpful to practise the right hand technique without changing chords, to get used to the feel you are trying to

achieve. Also, the plectrum strokes are quite choppy, so that the notes don't ring out for too long. You may find it easier at first with a light plectrum until you get used to it.

On one set of tunes, I play a strum in a variation of a Samba rhythm. This is explained in the notes that accompany the tunes. (Listen to *Music in the glen*).

4 Fingerpicked chords

This style is particularly suitable for slow reels and hornpipes, *especially on nylon strung guitar*. It sounds very mellow, because of the nylon strings and because the plectrum is not being used. It also sounds more like piano accompaniment, because of both the staccato (clipped) way the chords are played and the choice of chords used. I play two different patterns in this style.

The first is basically a fingerpicked bass and chord pattern, using the thumb and first/second fingers. If the same chord is played for a bar, (four beats), I sometimes play a bass note on the first beat only and the rest of the chord on beats 2, 3 and 4. Alternatively, I may pick out single notes from the chord on beats 2, 3 and 4. If the chord changes within the bar, I generally play bass-chord-bass-chord. (Listen to *Cooley's hornpipe* & *The home ruler*).

The second pattern bears a resemblance to the Shetland style of piano accompaniment, where the root and sometimes also the tenth (third) of the chord are played on the beat (measures one and three of the bar) and another note of the chord is played on the offbeat (measures two and four of the bar). (Listen to *Pretty Peg* & *The baker*).

I prefer the sound of this style on nylon-string guitar but don't be afraid to try it out on steel strings. The examples written in TAB with the tunes played in this style should help you to grasp this style.

5 Plectrum-picked chords

Sometimes I mix a strumming style with a plectrum picked style, especially in DADGAD. (Listen to *Mist-covered mountain* & *The rakes of Kildare*).

This technique is not unlike the bluegrass style known as crosspicking, where the plectrum is used to pick out the notes of a chord in an alternating up and down pattern to create a fast fingered-picked sound. I play two versions of this style. One version is explained in detail in the section on DADGAD. (Listen to *Doctor O'Neill* & *Mug of brown ale*, *Mist-covered mountain* & *Trip to Athlone*). The other style is used in standard tuning, on *Julia Delaney*. It involves a similar technique; because of the tuning and the chords used, the flavour is quite different.

Photo: Irene Young

Dennis Cahill

3·3 Tunings

I present four tunings and they range from standard tuning to DADGAD, dropping one string at a time, like this:

1 Standard tuning: E-A-D-G-B-E

> Always try to get perfectly in tune; get a friend to tune the guitar, buy an electronic tuner, train your ears and *listen*

2 Dropped D: D-A-D-G-B-E

> To tune to this tuning, lower the 6th string until it is in tune with the 5th string, 5th fret.

3 Double dropped D: D-A-D-G-B-D

> To tune to this tuning from standard tuning, lower the 6th string until it is in tune with the 5th string, 5th fret, then lower the 1st string until it is in tune with the 2nd string, 3rd fret.

4 DADGAD: D-A-D-G-A-D

> To tune to this tuning from standard tuning, lower the 1st string until it is in tune with the 2nd string, 3rd fret, then lower the 2nd string until it is in tune with the 3rd string, 2nd fret. Then, lower the 6th string until it is in tune with the 5th string, 5th fret.

Alternative tunings came to be used by accompanists to Irish music presumably because it was felt that standard tuning did not offer enough in the way of harmonic sympathy and scope for rhythmic experimentation with Irish tunes. Since many of the tunes are in the key of D, it makes sense to have the sixth string tuned down to D, to allow a full six-string D chord to be played. All of the altered tunings I present have the sixth string tuned down to D.

1 **Dropped D (DADGBE)** is used in many other styles, notably in blues slide guitar. Any chord shapes from standard tuning not using the sixth string can still be used, and ones using the sixth string can be modified to allow for the lowered note.

2 **Double Dropped D (DADGBD)** is the most recent of these tunings to be used in Irish music. It offers a mid-ground between Dropped D and DADGAD. If you like the modal sound of having lots of open D strings but miss the harmonic fullness of the other tunings, I suggest you experiment with this tuning.

3 **DADGAD** became popular for a few reasons. Firstly, because it has three open D strings, it very easy to find pleasant sounding chords for accompanying tunes in D. Thanks to the capo, once you learn a few chords in D, they are instantly useable in several different keys. In turn, this means that the player can focus on the rhythms, which is a crucial element of accompaniment.

As you can see, each of the tunings has their strengths and weaknesses. Many players don't settle exclusively on one but use different tunings for different effects and in different situations. For example, you'll find that the dropped D tunings are very suitable for driving rhythms. For playing with a lighter touch, you may like DADGAD and so on.

Session in Cleary's bar, Miltown Malbay, County Clare
Left to right: John Kelly (fiddle), Ian Roome (guitar) and Joe Ryan (fiddle)

Photo: Tony C Kearns

© 2000 Dave Mallinson Publications

With all of these rhythms, practise the right-hand technique without changing chords to get used to the feel you are trying to achieve.

You may find it easier at first with a light plectrum, until you get used to it. It may take a while to get the rhythm to sound smooth but rest assured that the more you do it, the smoother it will become.

If it doesn't come naturally, experiment with different angles of the plectrum to the strings, different plectrum gauges and different positions along the strings. These will all affect the tone and the rhythm of your playing.

The tunes in this book

The next section has a lot of information, so please take your time in reading it. The tunes on the soundtrack are all recorded in twos and with a few exceptions, each tune is played twice. In all cases, I have written 8 bars of chords per line, which means that in most cases, 4 lines of chords covers the tune once round. For ease of reference, I have labelled each part as follows;

A1, A2, B1 and B2 represent each corresponding part of the first time round the tune.

A3, A4, B3 and B4 represent the parts of the second time round the tune.

Any chords or chord sequences that have been referred to in the text are highlighted in the chord chart.

Because I was trying to demonstrate as many chord sequences, etc, as possible, the accompaniment may sound cluttered and 'busy' in some places. Please bear this in mind when listening and form your own judgement as to how much you would use in the course of any particular tune. Also, the variations I use on the second time round some of the tunes demonstrate that there is generally more than one set of chords for a tune; as your ears develop harmonically, you will begin to hear how you can give a tune a different flavour without sounding 'wrong'. Also, if you play with the same players regularly, you will soon become familiar with the way they phrase the tunes and you'll develop empathy as an accompanist. When listening to the soundtrack, listen especially for moving bass lines, which feature on many tracks.

Photo: Tony C Kearns

Arty McGlynn

Photo: Ron Hill

Ed Boyd

3·4 Tunes accompanied in standard tuning

JOHN BRADY'S & HEXHAM RACES

Tuning:	EADGBE
Type of tune:	jigs
Key on recording:	Bm & A
Key in book and capo position:	Am (capo 2) & A (no capo)
Right hand pattern:	steady strum

Rhythmically I use a two bar pattern, as shown in *Figure 5.*

Figure 5: Right hand rhythm in JOHN BRADY'S & HEXHAM RACES

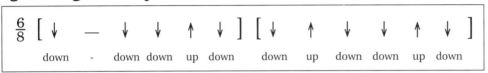

$$\frac{6}{8} \left[\downarrow \quad - \quad \downarrow \quad \downarrow \quad \uparrow \quad \downarrow \right] \left[\downarrow \quad \uparrow \quad \downarrow \quad \downarrow \quad \uparrow \quad \downarrow \right]$$

down - down down up down down up down down up down

In A1 and A2 of *John Brady's,* one chord is played, an Am, which has no third in it and is sometimes referred to as a *modal chord.* (See appendix). After this, I use two descending chord progressions, made up of chords as in *Figure 6.*

The last chord in the first tune, D/F♯ (E/G♯ without the capo), helps to make the key change from Bm to A. Note the effect of the key change; I like the drop of a whole step while also going from minor to major.

In *Hexham races* I continue with the same rhythm pattern. I make liberal use of an ascending progression, made up of the chords shown in *Figure 7.*

If you learn to play these chords in this order, what you hear in the accompaniment will make sense very quickly and

you'll find uses for these chord progressions in many tunes. When playing A/C♯ or Bm7, you can damp the fifth string with whatever finger is fretting the sixth string.

Have a listen for the rhythm triplet in the last bar of A3 (of *Hexham races*), on an E7 chord. Three beats are played in the space of beats 1 and 2 of the bar.

Figure 6

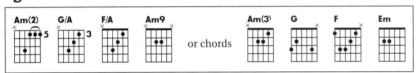

Am(2) G/A F/A Am9   or chords   Am(3) G F Em

Figure 7

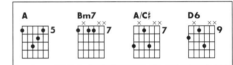

A Bm7 A/C♯ D6

JOHN BRADY'S, capo 2

A1	Am	(1)	Am		Am		Am		Am		Am		Am		Am	
A2	Am		Am		Am		Am		Am		Am		Am		Am	
B1	Am	(2)	Am	G/A	Am		Am	G/A	Am		Am	G/A	F/A	Am9	Am9	
B2	Am	(3)	Am		Am		Am	G	Am		Am	G	F	Em	Em	—

A3	Am	(2)	Am	G/A	Am		Am	G/A	Am		G/A		F/A		Am9	
A4	Am	(3)	Am	Em	Am		Am	Em	F		Em		F		Em	Am
B3	Am	(2)	Am	G/A	Am		Am	G/A	Am		G/A		F/A	Am9	Am9	
B4	Am	(3)	Am	Em	Am		Am	Em	Am		Am	G	F		F	D/F♯

HEXHAM RACES, no capo

A1	A		A		A		Bm7	E7	A		A		A		Bm7	E7
A2	A		A		A		Bm7	E7	A		Bm7	A/C♯	D6		E7	
B1	A		A		A		Bm7	E7	A		A		D6		E7	
B2	A		A	Bm7	A/C♯		Bm7	E7	A		A	A/C♯	D6		E7	

A3	A		Asus		A		Bm7	E7	A		Bm7	A/C♯	D6		E7	
A4	A		Bm7		A/C♯		Bm7	E7	A		A	A/C♯	D6		E7	
B3	A		A	Bm7	A/C♯		Bm7	E7	A		A		D6		E7	
B4	A		A	Bm7	A/C♯		Bm7	E7	A		Bm7	A/C♯	D6	Bm7	E7	A

Am(1) Am(2) G/A F/A Am9 Am(3) G F Em D/F♯ A Bm7 E7 A/C♯ D6 Asus

© 2000 Dave Mallinson Publications

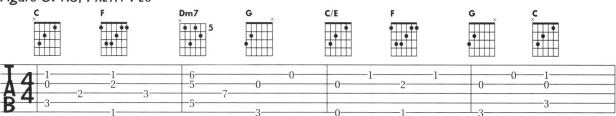

TRACKS 11 & 37

PRETTY PEG & THE BAKER

Tuning:	EADGBE
Type of tune:	Scotch reels
Key on recording:	D & A
Key in book and capo position:	C & G (capo 2)
Right hand pattern:	fingerpicked chords for nylon guitar

These two Scottish tunes have a slightly different structure to most of the other tunes in this book, in that the parts are only four bars long. Therefore, each line of chords contains either both A parts, or both B parts and the tune repeats after two lines of chords. The tunes are played three times each, as they are short.

Though the tunes are in D and A, I've chosen to use a capo on the second fret and play using the keys of C and G, respectively. You might find it easiest to learn the right hand technique via the TAB examples I have given in *Figures 8* & *9* below. Please note that some of the chords used here are chosen for this style and may not sound right if strummed. Also, you may notice that I am fingering strings that I'm not playing; this is so that the right hand choice of strings does not have to be totally accurate. With the right hand, use the thumb for the fourth, fifth and sixth strings.

About the chords

To play an alternating bass line on a C chord, you can switch your third finger between the fifth and sixth strings, third fret, instead of having both strings fretted all the time.

Figure 8: A6, PRETTY PEG

Figure 9: B5, THE BAKER

PRETTY PEG, capo 2

A1/A2 C	C G/B	C	F G	C	Dm7 G	C/E F	G/C G
B1/B2 C	C F	C	D7 G	C	C/E F	C	F G
A3/A4 C	C G	C	C G	C F	Dm7 G	C/E F	G a b
B3/B4 C	C F	C	F G	C	C/E F	C/E	F G
A5/A6 C	C G	C	C G	C F	Dm7 G	C/E F	G C
B5/B6 C	C F	C Am7	D7 G	C	C F	C Am7	D7 G

THE BAKER, capo 2

A1/A2 G	D7/A D7	G	D7/A D7	G G/B	D7/A D7	G G/B	C D7
B1/B2 G G/B	D7/A D7	G G/B	C D7	G G/B	D7/A	G/B	C D7
A3/A4 G G/B	D7/A D7	G	C D7 G	G G/B	D7/A D7	G G/B	C D7
B3/B4 G	D7/A	G/B	C D7	G G/B	D7/A D7	G G/B	C D7 G
A5/A6 G	D7/A	G/B	C D7	G G/B	D7/A D7	G G/B	C D7
B5/B6 G	D7/A D7	G G/B	C D7	G G/B	C D7	G G/B	C D7 G

C

G/B

F

G

Dm7

C/E

Am7

D7/A

D7

© 2000 Dave Mallinson Publications

FLOGGING REEL & THE WHISTLING POSTMAN

Tuning:	EADGBE
Type of tune:	reels
Key on recording:	G & A
Key in book and capo position:	G & A (no capo)
Right hand pattern:	Shetland swing

Spend as long as it takes to get comfortable with these chords if the shapes are new to you. Check out the suggestions on developing a practice routine; believe me, it will come with practice.

The *Flogging reel* has three parts, each part being four bars long. The structure of the tune is A-A-B-B-C-C. The chords for each part are almost identical. Note the use of an upstroke in the last bar of B1 in *The flogging reel*.

The *postman* is a regular two-part tune, with an A-A-B-B structure.

Note that the chords used are totally based on two very similar four-bar chord progressions. This demonstrates how versatile some of these chords are. The two progressions are shown in their basic form in *Figures 10 & 11*.

Figure 10: First chord progression, THE WHISTLING POSTMAN

| A | / | A/C♯ | / | D6 | / | Bm7 | / | A/C♯ | / | Cdim | / | Bm7 | / | E7 | / |

Figure 11: Second chord progression, THE WHISTLING POSTMAN

| A | / | A/C♯ | / | D | / | Bm7 | / | A/C♯ | / | D | / | E7 | / | / | / |

FLOGGING REEL, no capo

A1/A2	G	D7/A	G/B	C6	G/B		Am7	D7	G	D7/A	G/B	C6	G/B		Am7	D7
B1/B2	G	D7/A	G/B	C6	G/B		Am7	D7	G	D7/A	G/B	C6	G/B		Am7	D7
C1/C2	G		G		Dm		Dm	G	G	D7/A	G/B	C6	G/B		Am7	D7
A3/A4	G	D7/A	G/B	C6	G/B	Em7	Am7	D7	G	D7/A	G/B	C6	G/B		Am7	D7
B3/B4	G	D7/A	G/B	C6	G/B		Am7	D7	G	D7/A	G/B	C6	G/B		A/C♯	D7
C3/C4	G		G		Dm		Dm	G	G	D7/A	G/B	C6	G/B		Am7	E7

THE WHISTLING POSTMAN, no capo

A1	A	E7/B	A/C♯	D6	A/C♯		Bm7	E7	A	A/C♯	D6	Bm7	A/C♯	D6	E7
A2	A	A/C♯	D6	Bm7	A/C♯	Cdim	Bm7	E7	A	A/C♯	D	Bm7	A/C♯	D	E7
B1	A	A/C♯	D6	Bm7	A/C♯	Cdim	Bm7	E7	A	A/C♯	D	Bm7	A/C♯	D	E7
B2	A	A/C♯	D6	Bm7	A/C♯	Cdim	Bm7	E7	A	A/C♯	D	Bm7	A/C♯	D	E7
A3	A	A7/G	D/F♯	D	A/C♯	Cdim	Bm7	E7	A	A/C♯	D	Bm7	A/C♯	D	E7
A4	A	A/C♯	D6	Bm7	A/C♯	Cdim	Bm7	E7	A	A/C♯	D	Bm7	A/C♯	D	E7
B3	A	A/C♯	D6	Bm7	A/C♯	Cdim	Bm7	E7	A	A/C♯	D	Bm7	A/C♯	D	E7
B4	A	A/C♯	D6	Bm7	A/C♯	Cdim	Bm7	E7	A	A/C♯	D	Bm7	A/C♯	D	E7	A

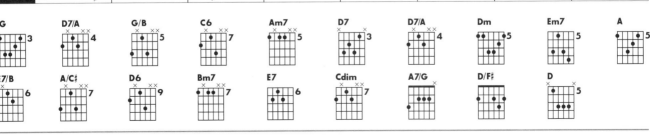

© 2000 Dave Mallinson Publications

TRACKS 2 & 28

PIGEON ON THE GATE & THE SHASKEEN REEL

Tuning:	EADGBE
Type of tune:	reels
Key on recording:	Em & G
Key in book and capo position:	Em & G (no capo)
Right hand pattern:	bass strum

You should find the backing on these tunes straightforward enough if you are familiar with some basic chords. The first time round the *Pigeon on the gate* uses only two chords, Em and Dmaj9, on the top four strings. This demonstrates how you can add sparse accompaniment effectively.

If you use the suggested fingering shown below, you'll find you can keep your little finger (fourth) on the third string ninth fret for both chords, thereby acting as an anchor between the two chords. Rhythmically, a very light strum is played on the top four strings, playing two plectrum strokes for each beat in a down-up pattern.

In the second time round the tune I incorporate all six strings into a full version of the same rhythm. At the beginning of each phrase, I often leave out the up-stroke in the 'and' of the first beat to create a sort of bounce in the rhythm. For example, listen to A4, bars 1, 3, and 5.

The chord patterns used here are very versatile; you'll find that they fit in many E minor tunes. In particular, the Em-A7-D-Bm progression forms the structure of the pattern and the G and D/F♯ are less pivotal but provide further movement to the bass line.

In *The Shaskeen reel*, I make use of moving bass lines all the way through. Some of the chord names may be confusing, as the only important note is the bass note (e.g. in D/F♯, F♯ is the bass note—see appendix: chord theory under slash chords). The second chord played, G/A is really just a passing note of A, played as a stepping stone for the bass from G to B. In B1 and B3, I use two alternating chords (G/D and Gsus/D) against a drone on the D string, to create a break from the rolling-along effect of the bass lines. In some places, I just play bass notes in place of chords; these are written as lower case letters and are played on the fifth or sixth string.

PIGEON ON THE GATE, no capo

A1	Em	Em	Dmaj9	Dmaj9	Em	Em	Dmaj9	Dmaj9
A2	Em	Em	Dmaj9	Dmaj9	Em	Em	Dmaj9	Dmaj9
B1	Em	Em	Dmaj9	Dmaj9	Em	Em	Dmaj9	Dmaj9
B2	Em	Em	Dmaj9	Dmaj9	Em	Em	Dmaj9	Dmaj9

A3	Em	Em A7	D G	D/F♯ Bm	Em	Em A7	D G	Bm Em
A4	Em	Em A7	D G	D/F♯ Bm	Em	Em A7	D G	Bm Em
B3	Em	Em A7	D	D/F♯	Em	Em G	D/F♯ G	Bm Em
B4	Em	Em A7	D	Bm	Em	Em A7	D G	Bm Em

THE SHASKEEN REEL, no capo

A1	G G/A	G/B C	G Em	Am7 D	G G/A	G/B C	D	D e f♯
A2	G G/A	G/B C	G/B	C D	G G/A	G/B C	D	e f♯ g
B1	G/D	Gsus/D	G/D Gsus/D	G/D Gsus/D	G/D	Gsus/D	Gsus/D	Gsus/D G/D
B2	G	D/F♯	G Em	Am D	G G/A	G/B C	D	D e f♯

A3	G G/A	G/B C	G Em	Am7 D	G G/A	G/B C	D	D e f♯
A4	G G/A	G/B C	G Em	Am7 D	G G/A	G/B C	D	D D/F♯
B3	G/D	Gsus/D	G/D Gsus/D	G/D Gsus/D	G/D	Gsus/D	Gsus/D	Gsus/D G/D
B4	G/D	Gsus/D	G/D D	G/D D	G/D D	Em D	C G/B	a f♯ G -

Opening chords

Em Dmaj9 Em A7 G D/F♯ Bm G/A G/B C Am7 G/D Gsus/D D

3·5 Tunes accompanied in dropped D (DADGBE)

*T*his tuning is just what it says, standard tuning but with the sixth string tuned down one tone (or whole step) to D. You can tune the sixth string by fretting the fifth string at the fifth fret and tuning to this note.

Having D as the lowest note opens up several options.

1 It enables fuller sounding D chords—a six-string version of D can now be played with the root on the bass. Many tunes are in D, so this makes for a fatter sounding accompaniment.

2 Also, when playing in D or G, it's possible to play bass note lines going down to D.

I present three different approaches to playing in this tuning.

1 Steady strum

Track 12

Fred Finn's & *Music in the glen*

2 Plectrum-picked chords

Track 4

Julia Delaney & *My love is in America*

3 Fingerpicked chords

Track 13

Cooley's hornpipe & *The home ruler*

With this tuning, you will have to modify many of the chords used in standard tun-ing to take the lower D string into account. Thankfully, you can accompany Irish tunes effectively with a limited repertoire of chords and most of the chords are just altered slightly. What's more, the learning experience will help increase your understanding of the guitar fingerboard.

Because this tuning lends itself to full bodied chords, it is well suited to a right hand rhythm which drives the tune along, by a strum which covers all six strings. However, you may find that leaving out the first string (either by damping or by not hitting it) gives a smoother sound.

Photo: David J Taylor

Session in Jimmy Burke's, Ardrahan, County Galway
Left to right: Eilish O'Connor (fiddle), Marion McCarthy (pipes) and Frank Kilkelly (guitar)

Photo: Patty Bronson

Dáithí Sproule

Mark Kelly

© 2000 Dave Mallinson Publications

FRED FINN'S & MUSIC IN THE GLEN

TRACKS 12 & 38

Tuning:	DADGBE
Type of tune:	reels
Key on recording:	D & G
Key in book and capo position:	D & G (no capo)
Right hand pattern:	steady strum

The accompaniment starts with some triads (3-note chords) played in a Samba-style rhythm on the top 3 strings, with a constant D drone going on the open fourth string. There are 5 chords used but only 3 different shapes. See *Figure 12.* These chords are only used for the first time round *Fred Finn's.*

The Samba rhythm

The rhythm pattern here may take a bit of getting used to. You can either try getting it by feel or you can slow it right down and work out the pattern. To help you, the pattern for one bar of $\frac{4}{4}$ is shown in *Figure 13.*

Count this very slowly, say the '1 and 2 and 3 and 4 and' out loud and tap out the rhythm; you'll soon get the hang of it. As you can see, the second and third measures are on the off beat, i.e., they're on the 'and' rather than the top of the beat. When comfortable with it, you can add extra little strums into the gaps, as you can hear I have done on the recording.

On the second time round the tune, the strumming pattern breaks into a fuller rhythm using constant down-up strokes but with the emphases in the same places. This means that the down beat on the 'and'

of 3 must become an up beat.

The chords are based on the bottom four strings; occasionally the rhythm is pushed around, placing emphasis on the offbeats. Also, it's played on the beat now and again, spiking it a bit further.

Music in the glen continues in the same rhythmic flavour. Note that I use a descending progression in A1 bars 3 and 4, (C, Bm7, Am7) and in A2, I reverse it, (making it ascend) and it still fits!

In the chord charts, I have used markers to show places where there are two chords in the bar but they do not share the bar equally.

Figure 12: the chords in FRED FINN'S

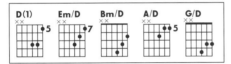

D(1)   Em/D   Bm/D   A/D   G/D

Figure 13: the Samba rhythm

1	and	2	and	3	and	4	and
down			up		down		

FRED FINN'S, no capo

A1	D(1)	D	Em/D	Em/D	D	D	Em/D	Em/D
A2	D(1)	D	Em/D	Em/D	D	D	Em/D	Em/D
B1	D(1)	D	Bm/D	Bm/D / /A/D	D	D	G/D	A/D
B2	D(1)	D	Bm/D	G/D A/D	D	D	G/D	A/D

A3	D(2)		D	Em G	D A	D	D	G	A
A4	D		D	Em G	D A	D	D	G	A
B3	D	G	D/F♯	Bm7	G A	D	D	G	A
B4	D	G	D	Bm7 / / D/F♯	G A	D	D	G	A D

MUSIC IN THE GLEN, no capo

A1	G	G	C Bm7	Am7 D	G	G	C	D
A2	G	G	Am7 Bm7	C D	G	G	C	D
B1	G / / C Bm7 Am7	G	Am7 D	G / / Bm7 C D	Em / / Bm7 Am7 D			
B2	G	G D/F♯	G	Am7 D	G / / Bm7 C D	Em / / Bm7 Am7 D		

A3	G	G	C	D	G	G	C	D
A4	G	G	C Bm7	Am7 D	G	G	C	D
B3	G C	Bm7 Am7	G	Am7 D	G	Am7 D	Em	Am7 D
B4	G	G D/F♯	G	Am7 D	G	Am7 D	Em Bm7	Am7 D

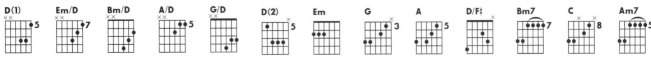

D(1)   Em/D   Bm/D   A/D   G/D   D(2)   Em   G   A   D/F♯   Bm7   C   Am7

© 2000 Dave Mallinson Publications

JULIA DELANEY & MY LOVE IS IN AMERICA

Tuning:	DADGBE
Type of tune:	slow reel & reel
Key on recording:	Dm & D
Key in book and capo position:	Dm & D (no capo)
Right hand pattern:	plectrum picked chords & steady strum

Julia Delaney is a very unusual and rhythmically complex tune, in that the pulse doesn't fall on the top of the bar, for the A part; it falls on the third beat, half way through the bar. On the recording, the first note that the accordion plays is on the first beat of the bar, so you should count through the beats starting on that note. I've chosen to follow the pulse with the accompaniment, so the guitar comes in half way through the first bar. On the B part, the pulse returns to its normal position on the first beat of the bar. It may take a few listens to figure out what's going on in the tune.

The guitar starts this set with an introduction and the chords I use are also used throughout the accompaniment for the first tune. The introduction is shown as the first line in the chord chart and there are two extra beats of silence between the introduction and the start of the tune.

The first time round the tune, I use a sequence of chords fingering only the second and third strings. All of the slash chords (see appendix for an explanation of slash chords) in the first tune are played with an open D on the fourth string. To demonstrate the right hand technique I have written out the introduction in TAB in *Figure 14.*

Refer to page 13 for information on the right hand style used here. The timing here is not written accurately, you will have to work it out from listening to the recording.

The rhythm picks up in *My love is in America*, with a slight pause after the first beat in the bar in the early stages. Otherwise, the rhythm is a constant down-up stroke with a slight emphasis on the bass notes of new chords. I play an occasional downstroke on the second beat, as you can hear in bars 2 of B2 and A4. Listen for the hammer-on (onto C♯) in the last bar of A3. A popular device is to join in the rhythm at the end of the tune, as I do here in the last two bars.

Figure 14: Intro, JULIA DELANEY

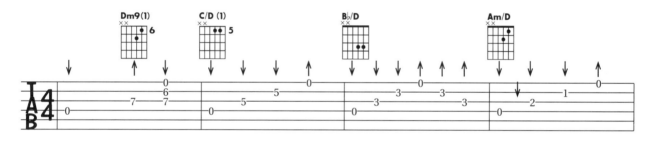

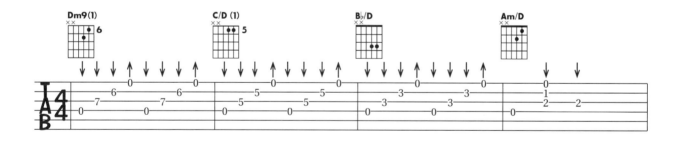

© 2000 Dave Mallinson Publications

Photo: Richard Faulks

Ian Carr

Photo: David Katzenstein

John Doyle

JULIA DELANEY, no capo

	Dm9(1)	C/D(1)	Bb/D	Am/D	Dm9(1)	C/D(1)	Bb/D	Am/D
A1	/ / Dm9(2)	C/D(2) Dm9(1)	/ / Dm9(2)	C/D(2) Dm9(1)	/ / Dm9(2)	C/D(2) Dm9(1)	/ / Dm9(2)	C/D(2) Dm9(1)
A2	/ / Dm9(1)	C/D(1) Bb/D	/ / Dm9(1)	C/D(1) Bb/D	/ / Dm9(1)	C/D(1) Bb/D	/ / Dm9(1)	C/D(1) Bb/D
B1	Dm9(1)	C/D(1)	Bb/D	Am/D	Dm9(1)	C/D(1)	Bb/D Am/D	Am/D
B2	Dm9(1)	C/D(1)	Bb/D	Am/D Bb/D	Dm9(1)	C/D(1)	Bb/D Am/D	Am/D
A3	/ / Bb	C G(1)	/ / Bb	C G(1)	/ / Bb	C G(1)	/ / Bb	Am7 G(1)
A4	/ / Bb	C G(1)	/ / Bb	C G(1)	/ / Bb	C G(1)	/ / Bb	Am7 D
B3	Dm9(1)	C/D(1)	Bb/D	Am/D Bb/D	Dm9(1)	C/D(1)	Bb/D Am/D	Am/D Bb/D
B4	Dm9(1)	C/D(1)	Bb/D	Am/D Bb/D	Dm9(1)	C/D(1)	Bb/D Am/D	Am/D

MY LOVE IS IN AMERICA, no capo

A1	D	A7sus	D	G/B A7	D	D	G/B	G/B A7
A2	D	G/B	D	G/B A7	D	D	G(2) D/F♯	G(2) A7/E
B1	D	D G/B	D	G(1)	D	D	D	G(1) A7
B2	D	D G/B / /	D	G(1) A	D A7/E	D/F♯	G(2) D/F♯	G(2) / / A7/E
A3	D	A7sus	D	G/B A7	D	D	G(1) D/F♯	Em7 A7/C♯
A4	D	D G/B / /	D	G/B A7/C♯	D A7/E	D/F♯	G(2) D/F♯	G(2) A
B3	D	D	D	G(1) A	D A7/E	D/F♯	G(2) D/F♯	G(2) A
B4	D G/B	D	D	Em7 A	D A7/E	D/F♯	G(1) D/F♯	G(1) A
								D

Chord diagrams: Dm9(2) [10] C/D(2) [8] Bb C [3] G(1) [3] Am7 D A7sus G/B A7 G(2) [3] D/F♯ D/F♯ or A7/E Em7 A7/C♯ [2]

COOLEY'S HORNPIPE & THE HOME RULER

Tuning:	DADGBE
Type of tune:	hornpipes
Key on recording:	G & D
Key in book and capo position:	G & D (no capo)
Right hand pattern:	fingerpicked chords for nylon guitar

TRACKS 13 & 39

These are accompanied in a fingerstyle and I play the chords in a way similar to piano accompaniment where the root and tenth (or third) notes (See appendix) are played together on the on-beat (the first or third beat). The examples shown in TAB should be all you need to work out the pattern for the right hand. If you glance at the chord chart, you will see how versatile a small number of chord progressions can be.

Note that in bar 4 of A4 of *Cooley's*, I play an Am7, because the fiddler on the recording chose a variation (C) which would clash with A7/C♯, which I use in this place in the tune on every other occasion.

About the chords

D/F#(1) is used all through The home ruler except in bars 1 and 2 of A3, where D/F#(2) is used.

Some chord names may change depending on what notes are played. For example, the following chord could be D/F# or D, depending on what strings you play: D/F#

Figure 15: B1 bars 1 to 4, COOLEY'S HORNPIPE

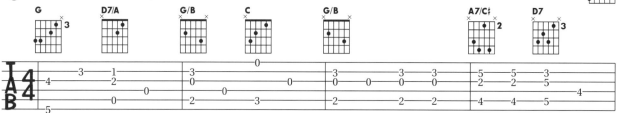

Figure 16: B1 bars 1 to 4, THE HOME RULER

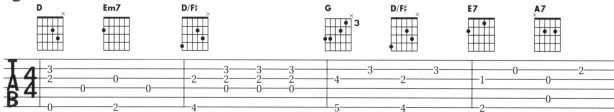

COOLEY'S HORNPIPE, no capo

A1	G	C	G		C G/B	A7/C♯ D7	G	C	G		C D7	G
A2	G	C	G		C G/B	A7/C♯ D7	G	C	G		C D7	G D G /
B1	G	D7/A	G/B C	G/B	A7/C♯ D7	G	C	C G	G	Am7	D7	G
B2	G	D7/A	G/B C	G/B	A7/C♯ D7	G	C	C G	G	Am7	D7	G

A3	G	D7/A	G/B	C	G/B	A7/C♯ D7	G	D7/A	G/B	C	D7	G C G/B Am7
A4	G	D7/A	G/B	C	G/B	Am7 D7	G	D7/A	G/B	C	D7	G C G/B Am7
B3	G	D7/A	G/B C	G/B	A7/C♯ D7	G	C	C G	Em7	Am7	D7	G
B4	G	D7/A	G/B C	G/B	A7/C♯ D7	G	C	C G	G	D7/A	D7	G A

THE HOME RULER, no capo

A1	D	Em7	D/F♯(1) G	D/F♯(1)	G	A	D	Em7	D/F♯(1) G	A			D
A2	D	Em7	D/F♯(1) G	D/F♯(1)	G	A	D	Em7	D/F♯(1) G	A			D G D/F♯(1) A
B1	D	Em7	D/F♯(1)	G	D/F♯(1)	E7	A7	D	Em7	D/F♯(1)	G	A	D
B2	D	Em7	D/F♯(1)	Em7 D/F♯(1)	G	A	D	G/B	D	D/F♯(1)	G	A /	G

A3	D/F♯(2) Dsus	D/F♯(2) Dsus	D	Bm7	E7	A7	D	Em7	D/F♯(1) G	A			D G D/F♯(1) A
A4	D	Em7	D/F♯(1) G	D/F♯(1) Bm7	E7	A7	D	Em7	D/F♯(1) G	A			D G D/F♯(1) A
B3	D	Em7	D/F♯(1)	Em7 D/F♯(1)	G	A	D	Em7	D/F♯(1)	G		A	D
B4	D	Em7	D/F♯(1)	Em7 D/F♯(1)	G	A	Bm7	A7/C♯	D	G	Em7	A7	D

Chord diagrams: G · C · G/B · A7/C♯ · D7 · D7/A · Am7 · A · D · Em7 · D/F♯(1) · E7 · A7 · D/F♯(2) · Bm7 · Dsus

© 2000 Dave Mallinson Publications

3·6 Tunes accompanied in double dropped D (DADGBD)

EDDIE KELLY'S JIG & JERRY'S BEAVER HAT

Tuning:	DADGBD
Type of tune:	jigs
Key on recording:	Em & D
Key in book and capo position:	Dm (capo 2) & D (no capo)
Right hand pattern:	steady strum

The rhythm I use for the accompaniment here fits in with the first two bars of the melody of *Eddie Kelly's jig*, in a pattern like that shown in *Figure 17*.

Before long, the space in the second beat is filled with an up-stroke and the rhythm thereafter is a regular down-up-down stroke pattern.

Chord changes are emphasised with a slightly heavier down-stroke and I shift the rhythmic emphasis in the highlighted bars in B3 to add dynamic variation. The chords are played on the sixth (last beat) before the bar where they fit and then continued through the bar where they belong. Moving the beat across the bar like this is called *syncopation*.

In *Jerry's beaver hat*, the rhythm continues in the same style. As I strum, the strings are damped, with the heel of the right hand. You may find it easier to try this style with a soft plectrum at first, until you get used to the feel of it.

Figure 17: Two bar rhythm pattern for EDDIE KELLY'S JIG

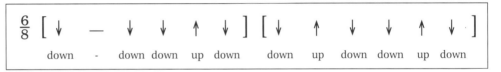

EDDIE KELLY'S JIG, capo 2

A1	Dm	Dm	Dm	Gm7	Am7	Dm	Dm	C	B♭	Am7	Am7
A2	Dm	Dm	Dm	Gm7	Am7	Dm	Dm	C	B♭	Am7	Am7
B1	Dm	Dm	Dm	Gm7	Am7	Dm	Dm	C	B♭	Am7	Am7
B2	Dm	Dm	Dm Gm7	Am7	Dm	Dm	Dm	C	B♭	Am7	Am7

A3	Dm	Dm	Dm	Gm7	Am7	Dm	Dm	C	B♭	Am7	Am7
A4	Dm	Dm Am7	Dm	Gm7	Am7	Dm	Dm	C	B♭	Am7	Am7
B3	Dm	Dm	Dm Gm7	Am7 / / / / B♭	B♭ / / / / Am7	Am7 / / / / B♭	Bb	Gm7	Am7		
B4	Dm	Dm	Dm	Gm7	Am7	Dm	Dm	C	Bb	Am7	Am7 Gm7

JERRY'S BEAVER HAT, no capo

A1	D	D G	D	G	A	D	D	G	D/F♯	A	D
A2	D	G	D/F♯	G	A	D	D	G	D/F♯	A	D
B1	D	G A	D	Em7	A	D	G	D/F♯	G	A	D
B2	D	G A	D	G	A	D	G	D/F♯	G	A	G/B A/C♯

A3	D	G	D/F♯	G	A	D	G		D/F♯	A	D
A4	D	G	D/F♯ Bm7	Em7	A	D	G		D/F♯	A	D
B3	D	G A	D	Em7	A	D	G	D/F♯	G	A	D
B4	D	G A	Bm7	E7	A	D	G	D/F♯	G	A	D

Dm   Gm7   Am7   C   B♭   D   G   A   D/F♯   Em7   G/B   A/C♯   Bm7   E7

© 2000 Dave Mallinson Publications

PIGTOWN FLING & ROLY-POLY

Tuning:	DADGBD
Type of tune:	reels
Key on recording:	G & D
Key in book and capo position:	D (capo 5) & D (no capo)
Right hand pattern:	Plectrum-picked chords & steady strum

TRACKS 8 & 34

Pigtown fling is a short tune as each part is only four bars long. Hence, it is played three times. It starts slowly with the guitar playing plectrum-picked chords and gathers tempo quickly. By the first B part, the guitar is strumming in a regular down-up pattern and emphases are placed on the bass note of each new chord. In the first bar of A4, I place an extra emphasis on the fourth beat of the bar. I do it again two bars later and again in the first

bar of A6. In the last bar of A6 the rhythm gets shifted in a different way. This time the emphasis is on the 'and' of the second beat. This falls on a upstroke and is repeated in the first bar of each of the remaining two B parts.

In the change to the next tune I moved the capo to its resting place behind the nut and you can hear the sliding action in the stop between the tunes.

In *Roly-poly,* I play damped

chords to start it off and the chords are played mainly on the bottom four strings. Physically, my hand is strumming up and down in the same pattern as before but I leave out some beats to create a syncopated feel. The basic emphases are shown in *Figure 18.*

In the third bar of B2, I play another rhythmic variation. Here, the emphasis is on the 'and' of the third beat, which is played on an upstroke.

Figure 18: The emphases in ROLY-POLY

1	and	2	*and*	3	and	*4*	and
down	up	down	*up*	down	up	*down*	up

PIGTOWN FLING, capo 5

A1/A2	D (1)	D Dsus	D/F♯ (1)	Dsus Asus/E	D	D Dsus	D/F♯ (1)	Dsus D/F♯ (1)
B1/B2	Bm	A7	Bm	Bm A7	Bm	A7	Bm	Bm A7

A3/A4	D (2)	D G/D	D	G A7	D / / D	D Dsus	D/F♯ (1) Dsus	Dsus
B3/B4	Bm	A (1)	G/A	G/A A	Bm	A	G/A	G/A A

A5/A6	D (1) G/D	D G	D/F♯ (2)	G A7	D / / D	D G	D/F♯	G A7
B5/B6	Bm	A7	G	G A7	Bm	A7	Em7 D/F♯	D/F♯ G -

ROLY-POLY, no capo

A1	D (3)	G	A (2)	A	D	G	A	A D
A2	D	G	A	A	D D/F♯ (2)	G	A	A D
B1	D	D	Em	G A	D	D	D/F♯ G	A D
B2	D	D	Em D/F♯	G A	D	D	D/F♯ G	A D

A3	D7	G	A	A	D/F♯	G	A	A D
A4	D D/F♯	G E7	A	A	D/F♯	G	A	A D
B3	D	D	Em7 D/F♯	G A	D	D	D/F♯ G	A D
B4	D	D	Em7 D/F♯	G A	D	D	D/F♯ G	A D

Chord diagrams: D(1) Dsus D/F♯(1) Asus/E Bm A7 D(2) G/D A(1) G/A G D/F♯(2) Em7 D(3) A(2) D7 E7

© 2000 Dave Mallinson Publications

3·7 Accompanying tunes in DADGAD

Chord names in DADGAD

Because of the nature of the tuning, many of the chords contain extra notes of the scale, (such as the fourth or the ninth) which means that their full titles can be unnecessarily complicated. For example, the G chord that I use most often has an A in it (the second and/or ninth note of the G scale) which technically makes the chord a major ninth. However, the abbreviated titles give enough information to tell you where these chords will fit in the tune.

This is the most popular alternative tuning used in folk guitar today. It was invented by Davy Graham and involves tuning the first, second and sixth strings one tone (or whole step) lower than standard tuning. To tune your guitar to this tuning:

1 Lower the first string until it is in tune with the second string fretted at the third fret;

2 Lower the second string until it is in tune with the third string fretted at the second fret and

3 Lower the sixth string until it is in tune with the fifth string fretted at the fifth fret.

Alternatively, you may find it easier to tune using the following method:

1 Lower the first string until it is in tune with the fourth string open;

2 Lower the second string until it is in tune with the fifth string open and

3 Lower the sixth string until it is in tune with the fourth string open.

There are many different rhythmic styles used by DADGAD players, from a light-fingered style (which is also used on bouzouki to accompany Irish music) which is not unlike bluegrass cross-picking to punchy, full-bodied aggressive rhythm. One of the great advantages of this tuning is the fact that there are three strings tuned to D and any or all of them can be allowed to ring unfingered through many of the chords to create a modal effect. By the same token, this limits the keys that are comfortable and a capo is an essential accessory for accompanying in this tuning.

I find DADGAD particularly suitable for jigs, which are in $\frac{6}{8}$ time. The pattern of right hand strokes (in a strumming pattern) is determined by the number of beats in the bar and in a jig the strum patterns shown in *Figure 19* will work well.

Figure 19: Strum patterns in jig time

	1st beat	2nd beat	3rd beat	4th beat	5th beat	6th beat
A	down ↓	skip	down ↓	up ↑	down ↓	up ↑
B	down ↓	up ↑	down ↓	up ↑	down ↓	up ↑
C	down ↓	up ↑	down ↓	down ↓	up ↑	down ↓

I like to use a plectrum-picked right hand style when accompanying jigs in DADGAD. This has a very light flavour. For example, listen to the accompaniment on the tunes in track 9, *Dr O'Neill* & *Mug of brown ale,* track 1, *Mist-covered mountain* and track 3, *Trip to Athlone.*

As you can hear, this style has a light feel and bears some resemblance to the style used by many Irish bouzouki players. Depending on your experience, you may find the right hand style a bit foreign at first. Bear in mind that you can slide over the strings with the plectrum rather than carefully picking out each note; it will have a similar effect. The following examples are played on tracks 15 to 26 of the soundtrack. Examples 1 to 3 use only a D chord.

Since many of the chords use only one or two fingers, this style lends itself to 'lines', i.e. a moving melody line that links the chords together. This will become clear as you follow the examples on the next few pages and listen to the appropriate tunes on the recording. *On the recording, the examples are introduced as Example 1, then Example 1 faster and so on.*

The first example shows a repeating down-up pattern using only the top four strings (Tracks 15 and 16).

Example 1   D

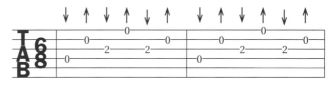

With this example and indeed with any rhythm, spend as much time as it takes to get completely comfortable with it, as it must sound smooth. When it does, you can begin to add some variations using *hammer-*

ons. A hammer-on is simply a way of getting two notes out of a string picked once. After the string has been played, you 'hammer-on' your ring finger onto the position where you want the second note. Try *Example 2,* using a

repeating down-up-down pattern but replacing the second beat with a hammer-on.

This example gives an arpeggio (or do-mi-so-do) feel which can be played quite fast to give a flowing, ringing sound.

Example 2   D(ho)

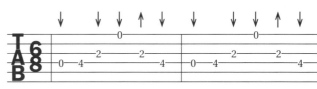

© 2000 Dave Mallinson Publications

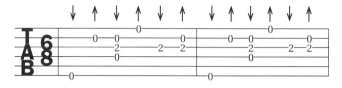

Example 3

To incorporate the six strings into this style start by trying *Example 3* (Tracks 19 and 20).

Once you get the feel of these rhythms you can loosen up your right hand and try hitting different strings. Being in an open tuning, more than likely it will sound OK! The basic rhythm might initially be easier to grasp using your index finger instead of a plectrum. Once you get the hang of the picking pattern, you can try it with the plectrum. Next, you need to learn a small handful of chords and chord progressions to enable you to use this style effectively and in the examples below I start you off with a few ideas for your own collection of DADGAD tricks and licks.

The next example (listen to Tracks 21 and 22) is a progression that I use a lot. You can hear it in bars 1 to 4 of B1 in *Trip to Athlone.* With the following examples, the chords change twice per bar, i.e., every three beats. You may notice that some of the chords have two names; these are known as *slash chords* (see appendix).

Example 4

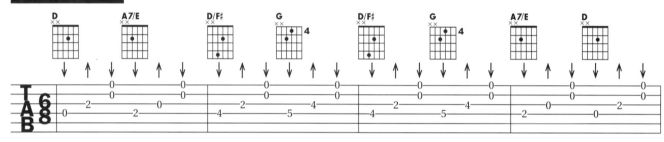

Example 5 can be heard in the last four bars of *The rakes of Kildare.* The picking pattern is basically a repeating down-up-down pattern. The most important feature of this progression is the descending bass line and if you play the chords I have given and play the bass notes in the right place, you'll be on the right track.

Example 5

Example 6 is another 'phrase' that I use often.

Example 6

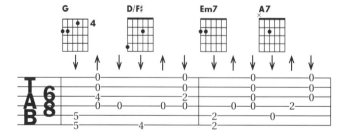

With these examples as a starting point, the secret is to experiment with different picking/strumming patterns and hammer-ons, pull-offs (a pull-off is the opposite to a hammer-on: a second note is sounded by pulling the finger off the string after you've just played the fretted note) and anything else you can think of to develop a style of your own.

If you're new to DADGAD, *Doctor O'Neill* (Track 9) is a good starting place, as it uses very few chord shapes.

 © 2000 Dave Mallinson Publications

3·8 Tunes accompanied in DADGAD

MIST-COVERED MOUNTAIN & THE RAKES OF KILDARE

Tuning:	DADGAD
Type of tune:	jigs
Key on recording:	Am & G
Key in book and capo position:	Dm (capo 7) & G (capo 5)
Right hand pattern:	Plectrum-picked chords & steady strum

These two lovely jigs are a good place to start if you're new to DADGAD. Spending some time with the examples in section 3·7 will be of help if this style is foreign to you.

On the first time round *Mist-covered mountain* the backing uses only two one-fingered chords, so this is a good place to get comfortable with the rhythm. The picking pattern described in section 3·7 on DADGAD is used here and for the second time round the rhythm becomes a full strum on all six strings, emphasising the chord changes with down strokes. The sequences of

chords used here will fit over many tunes in Dm and using the capo you can easily adapt them to other keys. A popular alternative would be capo 2, to play in Em.

The rhythm on *The Rakes of Kildare* is slightly heavier, with down-strokes covering all 6 strings announcing each new chord and a light strum filling in the spaces.

The pattern used is down-up-down down-up-down and occasionally (usually at the beginning of a phrase), I omit the second beat, allowing the first beat to ring on over the time of the second beat. In the

last four bars, I use a moving bass line that I find invaluable, so don't miss out on that! It is shown as *Example 5* on page 28.

About the chords

In the second bar of A3 in *Rakes of Kildare*, I use a hammer-on onto the F♯, playing the F♯ on the fourth string. Likewise, where I have used a hammer-on with A7/C♯, it is played with the third finger onto the fifth string fourth fret.

I start with a 4-string D chord but, as the tune progresses, I play all six strings with the same left-hand fingering.

MIST-COVERED MOUNTAIN, capo 7

A1	Dm	Dm	Am7	Am7	Dm	Dm	Am7	Am7
A2	Dm	Dm	Am7	Am7	Dm	Dm	Am7	Am7
B1	Dm	Dm	Am7	Am7	Dm	Dm	Am7	Am7
B2	Dm	Dm	Am7	Am7	Am7	Am7	Am7	Am7

A3	Dm	Dm G	C	C Am7	Dm	Dm G	C Am7	Am7 Dm
A4	Dm	Dm G	C	C Am7	Dm	Dm	B♭ Am7	Am7 Dm
B3	Dm	Dm G	C	C Am7	Dm	Dm	C Am7	Am7 Dm
B4	Dm	Dm G	C	C	C Am7	Am7	B♭ Am7	Am7 Dm

THE RAKES OF KILDARE, capo 5

A1	D	D	G	G A7	D	D	G A7	D
A2	D	D	G	G A7	D	D D/F♯	G A7	D
B1	D	D G	A7	A7	D	D G	A7	D
B2	D	D G	A7	A7	D	D D/F♯	G A7	D G

A3	D	D/F♯(ho)	G D/F♯	Em7 A7	D	D Bm7	G A7/C♯(ho)	D
A4	D	D G	Em7 D/F♯	G A7	D	D D/F♯	G A7	D
B3	D	D G	A7	G/B A7/C♯	D	D G	A7 A7/C♯	D
B4	D	D G	A7	G/B A7/C♯	D D/C♯	G/B D/A	G Em7	D

D or Dm	A7 or Am7	G	C	B♭	D/F♯	D/F♯(ho)	Em7	Bm7	A7/C♯(ho)	G/B	D/A	D/C♯

© 2000 Dave Mallinson Publications

DOCTOR O'NEILL & THE MUG OF BROWN ALE

Tuning:	DADGAD
Type of tune:	jigs
Key on recording:	D & Am
Key in book and capo position:	G (capo 7) & Dm (capo 7)
Right hand pattern:	Plectrum-picked chords

TRACKS 9 & 35

Here the focus is on the sound of some simple chords rather on than a driving rhythm. Practising the DADGAD examples on pages 27 and 28 will help you with the feel for the right hand. I chose to play with the capo at the seventh fret here, to show how you can play in the key of G using DADGAD. Also, because the second tune is in Am, it's not necessary to move the capo for the second tune: playing in the key of Dm with the capo on the seventh fret will give us the key of Am.

You may find it altogether easier to learn to play the chord shapes and then figure out how they are used by ear. I mentioned previously that using the full names for chords in DADGAD is somewhat redundant and this is particu-larly the case with the accompaniment for these jigs.

Doctor O'Neill is different from many other tunes in this book in that it has five parts, each played twice, giving a structure of A-A-B-B-C-C-D-D-E-E. Because of this, the tune is just played once. You can see from the chord windows, that I use the top 4 strings (the four nearest your knee) for the two A parts and then change to the bottom 4 strings (the four nearest your chin) for the rest of the tune.

The accompaniment for *The mug of brown ale* is also very sparse, with only slight varia-tions on each part. You'll find that I swap Am and C chords pretty much at random, that's because they are related (See Appendix, Chord theory on rel-ative minors). Note the effect of the G used at the start of the second time round the tune. This chord fits here because the melody of the tune has notes that belong to both Dm and G major scales.

About the chords

The D chord used here can also be called Dm; this is because there is no third in this chord, it can be used as either. Also, this chord is played with or without the fifth and sixth strings, depending on the preceding and following chords; use your ears to tell you which to play.

Also, note that G (1) is only used for the A-parts. The rest of the time, use G (2). The first four chords on the bottom of the page are the ones to use in the first two A parts.

DOCTOR O'NEILL, capo 7

A1	G (1)		D/F♯		C/E		C/E	D	G (1)		D/F♯		C/E		C/E	D
A2	G (1)		D/F♯		C/E		C/E	D/F♯	G (1)		D/F♯		C/E		C/E	D

B1	G (2)		G	D/A	G/D		C/D	D	G		G	D/A	G/D	C/D	D	G
B2	G		G	D/A	G/D		C/D	D	G		G	D/A	G/D	C/D	D	G

C1	G		G		C/D	G/D	C/D	D	G		G		C/D	Am7	D	G
C2	G		G		C/D	G/D	C/D	D	G		G		C/D	Am7	D	G

D1	G		G		G		C/D	D	G		G	G/D	C/D		G
D2	G	D	G/D		G/D		C/D	D	G		G	G/D	C/D		G

E1	G	C/D	G		G	D	G/D	C/D	G/D	C/D	G/D		C/D		G
E2	G	F	G		G/D	C/D	G/D	D	G/D	C/D	G		C/D		G

THE MUG OF BROWN ALE, capo 7

A1	Dm	Dm	Am7	Am7	Dm	Dm	Am7	Am7 Dm
A2	Dm	Dm	C	Am7	Dm	Dm	C	Am7 Dm
B1	Dm	Dm	Am7	C	Dm	Dm	Am7	Am7 Dm
B2	Dm	Dm	C	Am7	Dm	Dm	C	Am7

A3	G	G	Am7	Am7	G	G	Am7	C Dm
A4	Dm	Dm G	C	C Am7	Dm	Dm	Am7	Am7 Dm
B3	Dm	Dm	Am7	Am7	Dm	Dm	Am7	C Dm
B4	Dm	Dm	Am7	Am7	Dm	Dm	Am7	Am7 Dm

G (1)

D/F♯

C/E

D or Dm

G (2)

D/A

G/D

C/D

F

Am7

C

30

© 2000 Dave Mallinson Publications

THE TRIP TO ATHLONE & THE RAMBLING PITCHFORK

TRACKS 3 & 29

Tuning:	DADGAD
Type of tune:	jigs
Key on recording:	D & E
Key in book and capo position:	D (no capo) & D (capo 2)
Right hand pattern:	Plectrum-picked chords & steady strum

I use two different styles here. To vary the dynamics, I start with a plectrum-picked style which builds to a full strum and goes back to picking again for the start of the second tune.

On A1 and A2 of *The trip to Athlone*, I use a plectrum-picked style using only the top four strings. The first four chord windows (D, G, A7/E and D/F♯) are used here and none of these requires any more than two fingers of the left hand. This will give you a chance to concentrate on the style for the right hand. When playing chords D/F♯ and A/C♯, try using hammer-ons with the third finger onto the fourth and fifth strings respectively, as described in 3·7. You'll find they work well with these shapes—I have highlighted where they are used so you can hear the effect. Bars 1 to 4 of B1 are highlighted because they

are used as *Example 4*, page 28 in the DADGAD section.

I continue this style into the B parts but it builds in intensity until it becomes strummed chords by the fifth bar of B2. This continues into the second time round the tune, with a strum taking in all six strings and the chords are modified to finger any strings now being played. The 6-string version of the D, G, A7 and D/F♯ chords are used. The plectrum pattern used here is down-up-down down-up-down and occasionally (usually at the beginning of a phrase), I omit the second beat, allowing the first beat to ring on over the time of the second beat.

The rambling pitchfork is a very popular session tune but it's usually played in D. Many traditional musicians are playing old tunes in new keys, to give them a new lease of life. D

tunes often get moved up to E. This means that two tunes that have traditionally been played together can suddenly sound like a fresh pairing because of the new key of the second tune.

Dynamically, the accompaniment drops at the start of the new tune, reverting to the plectrum-picked style. Towards the end of A1 (bars 7 and 8) and into A2, I mingle plectrum-picked chords with strummed chords to build up the intensity again. The B-parts are played using strummed chords. On the second time round the tune, I ease up a little on the rhythmic intensity, in order to play hammer-ons.

About the chords

Use versions (1) or (2) of chords as directed: only the changes are indicated, e.g. start with D (1) and use it until directed to use D (2).

THE TRIP TO ATHLONE, capo 7

A1	D (1)	D	D	G (1) A7/E	D	D	G	G A7/E
A2	D	D	D	G A7/E	D	D	G	D/F♯ A7/E D
B1	D A7/E	D/F♯ G	D/F♯ G	A7/E D	C	G/B	C G/B	A/C♯ D
B2	D	D A7/E	D/F♯ G	A7/E D	C	G/B	C G/B	A/C♯ D

A3	D (2)	D G/B	D	G (2) A7	D	D	G	A7
A4	D	D G	D	Em7 A7	D	D	G	A7 D
B3	D	D Em7	D G	A7 D	C	G/B	C G/B	A/C♯ D
B4	D	D Em7	D/F♯ (2) G	A7 D	C	G/B	C G	A/C♯ D

THE RAMBLING PITCHFORK, capo 5

A1	D (2)	D	G (1) D/F♯ (1) A7/E A/C♯	D (1)	D	G (2)	A7
A2	D (2)	D D/F♯ (2)	G	G A7	D	D	G A7	D
B1	D	A7	D Em7	D/F♯ G	D/F♯	A7	G	D
B2	D	A7	D Em7	D/F♯ G	D/F♯	A7	G	G A/C♯

A3	D (1)	D D/F♯	G D/F♯	G A/C♯	D (2)	D	G A/C♯	D
A4	D/F♯	D/F♯	G	G A7	D	D D/F♯	G A7	D
B3	D	A7	D Em7	D/F♯ G	D/F♯	A7	G	D
B4	D	A7	D Em7	D/F♯ G	D/F♯	A7	G Em7	D

Chord diagrams: D(1) G(1) A7/E D/F♯(1) C G/B A/C♯ D(2) G A7 D/F♯(2) Em7

MY DARLING ASLEEP & BOYS OF THE TOWN

Tuning:	DADGAD
Type of tune:	jigs
Key on recording:	D & G
Key in book and capo position:	D (no capo) & D (capo 5)
Right hand pattern:	Steady strum

My darling asleep is accompanied on its first time through using only D, G and A. The focus here is on the rhythm, which is constant and drives the tune along. The rhythm pattern starts off as down-space-down down-up-down, i.e., the first beat of each bar is allowed to ring on a little. Since each new chord is played on either the first or fourth beat, they are always on down-strokes. The fourth beat is only emphasised if there is a new chord. (Refer to section 3·2 for more right hand ideas). On the second time through, the same chords are used for the most part but they are fleshed out in a few places with chord progressions, with the rhythm getting a little heavier handed.

In *Boys of the town,* the rhythm continues in the same style. Note that the chords for A2 are a repeat of A1 and likewise, the chords for A4 are a repeat of A3. This consistency helps to define the flavour of the tune.

About the chords

Some chords here have abbreviated titles, as their full names would make things unnecessarily complicated.

Session in McManus' pub, Dundalk, County Louth. Left to right: Gerry O'Connor (fiddle), Michael Feeley (flute), Donal O'Connor (fiddle), Eilish O'Connor, (fiddle) and Frank Kilkelly (guitar)

MY DARLING ASLEEP, no capo

A1	D		G		D		G	A7	D		G		D	G	A7	D
A2	D		G		D		G	A7	D		G		D	G	A7	D
B1	D		D		D		G	A7	D		G	A7	D	G	A7	D
B2	D		D	G	D		G	A7	D		G		D	G	A7	D

A3	D		G		D	G	Em7	A7	D		G		D	G	A7	D
A4	D		G		D/F♯	Bm7	Em7	A7	D		G		D	G	A7	D
B3	D		D	G	D		G	A7	D		G		D	G	A7	D
B4	D	Em7	D/F♯	G	D/F♯	Bm7	Em7	A7	D		G		D/F♯	G	A7	D

BOYS OF THE TOWN, capo 5

A1	D		D		D		G/D	A7	D		D		D	G/D	A7	
A2	D		D		D		G/D	A7	D		D		D	G/D	A7	
B1	D		G/D		D		G/D	A7	D		D	A7	G/D		A7	D
B2	D		A7		D		G/D	A7	D		D	A7	G/D		A7	A7/C♯

A3	D		D		D/F♯	G	D/F♯	A7	D		D		D/F♯	G	A7	
A4	D		D		D/F♯	G	D/F♯	A7	D		D		D/F♯	G	A7	
B3	D		G		D		G	A7	D		D	A7	G	Em7	A7	D
B4	D		D	G/D	D		G	A7	D		D	A7	G	Em7	A7	D

D   G   A7   Em7   D/F♯   Bm7   G/D   A7/C♯

32

© 2000 Dave Mallinson Publications

SHOEMAKER'S DAUGHTER & DINKIE'S REEL

TRACKS 14 & 40

Tuning:	DADGAD
Type of tune:	reels
Key on recording:	G & A
Key in book and capo position:	D (capo 5) & D (capo 7)
Right hand pattern:	Plectrum-picked chords & steady strum

The accompaniment to *Shoemaker's daughter* begins with some gentle plectrum-picked chords but before the end of A1, it becomes a strum, with the bass note of each new chord being emphasised with a slightly heavier downbeat. Hammer-ons are used abundantly here to retain a light feel. There is a slight pause on the D chord at the end of B2, to punctuate the repeat of the tune. I use a six-string D chord at the start of A3 and A4, to build the momentum very slightly.

I lighten up slightly going into *Dinkie's reel* to allow the new tune to announce its own arrival, as it were. The accompaniment here continues in the same vein as for the first tune.

In bars 1 to 3 of A3, I use an ascending chord progression; I use it again in with a different ending in bars 5 to 8 of A3. In bar 3 of A4, I emphasise a beat (other than the first beat) that is dominant in the melody; this can be an effective device. Also, in the last four bars of the set (bars 5 to 8 of B4) I feature a descending progression, which I use a lot.

SHOEMAKER'S DAUGHTER, capo 5

A1	D (1)	D Am7	D	D G (1)	D/F♯ (1)	D/F♯	D/F♯ D	Am7 D
A2	D (2)	D (1) Am7	D	D (ho) G	D (ho)	D	G D (ho)	G D
B1	D	D A7/E	D	D A7	D	D C	G/B	A7 (ho) D
B2	D (2)	D (1) A7	D	D A7 (ho)	D	D C	G/B	A7 (ho) D
A3	D (2)	D (1) A7 (ho)	D	D G	D	D	C G/B	A7 (ho) D
A4	D (2)	D (1) A7 (ho)	D	D G	D	D	C G/B	A7 (ho) D
B3	D (1)	D A7 (ho)	D	D A7 (ho)	D	D C	G/B	A7 (ho) D
B4	D (2)	D (1) A7/E	D	D A7 (ho)	D	D C	G/B	A7 (ho) D

DINKIE'S REEL, capo 7

A1	D	D	C	C A7 (ho)	D	D	C G/B	A7 (ho) D
A2	D (2)	D (1)	C	C A7 (ho)	D	D	C G/B	A7 D
B1	D (2)	D (1)	C	C	D	D	C G/B	A7 (ho) D
B2	D (2)	D (1)	C	C	D C	G/B A7	C G/B	A7 (ho) D
A3	D (2) Em7	D/F♯ (2) G (2)	Am7	Am7	D Em7	D/F♯ G	D/F♯ G	A7 (ho) D (1)
A4	D (2)	D (1)	C // G/B C	A7 (ho)	D	D	C G/B	A7 (ho) D
B3	D (2)	D (1)	C	C	D	D	C G/B	A7 (ho) D
B4	D (2)	D (1)	C	C	D C	G/B A7	G D/F♯	Em7 D (2)

Chord diagrams: D (1) | A7 or Am7 | G (1) | D/F♯ (1) | D (2) | D (ho) | A7/E | C | G/B | A7 (ho) | G (2) | D/F♯ (2) | Em7

© 2000 Dave Mallinson Publications

33

Section 4

4·0 APPENDIX

4·1 Theory

Chord Construction

Chords are derived from the scales on which they are based. By taking different combinations of notes out of the scales, we get different chords. Let's take the key of C.

The scale of C major, the *do-re-me*, consists of the notes C-D-E-F-G-A-B-C. The basic major chord comprises the notes C, E, G and C, i.e. the first (root), third, fifth and the eighth (root), notes of the scale. The eighth is the same note as the first or root but an octave higher and is sometimes omitted in explanations.

So, *Figure 20* shows how the main chords are derived from the scale in C.

Figure 20: **Chord construction**

Chord	root	2nd	3rd	4th	5th	6th	7th	root
Major	C		E		G			C
Minor	C		E♭		G			C
Minor 7th	C		E♭		G		B♭	
Major 7th	C		E		G		B	
7th or dominant	C		E		G		B♭	
Half-diminished	C		E♭		G♭		B♭	
Diminished	C		E♭		G♭		B♭♭(i.e.A)	
Suspended	C		F		G			C
Augmented	C		E		G♯			C

We can see from the chart that, for example, a minor seventh chord has a flattened (or minor) third and a flattened (or minor) seventh. These alterations to the major chord are what define any chord. If you find this difficult to grasp it may help to work at it in conjunction with a piano. The notes are linear on the keyboard so required knowledge is minimal and hearing the notes will certainly help.

So, there are four basic permutations of chords, depending on whether we have a major or minor third and a major or minor seventh.

1 Major third and major seventh:	major seventh (M7) chord, e.g., EM7
2 Major third and minor seventh:	seventh (7) chord, e.g. E7
3 Minor third and major seventh:	major minor seventh (Mm7), e.g. EMm7 (not very common)
4 Minor third and minor seventh:	minor seventh (m7) chord, e.g. Em7

34

© 2000 Dave Mallinson Publications

The following suggestion may seem like a very time-consuming exercise but I guarantee that if you work at it, your knowledge of the fingerboard and of chord theory will be greatly increased. I suggest you figure out why each chord in the book has the name it has.

To do this, pick a chord and use the appropriate guitar neck chart below to find a name for each note being played. Given the name of the chord, try to work out what position in the scale each note represents. For example, take an E minor (Em) chord in standard tuning: **Em**

We have:

String	condition	note	degree
sixth string	open	E	root
fifth string	second fret	B	fifth
fourth string	second fret	E	root
third string	open	G	third
second string	open	B	fifth
first string	open	E	root

Our ears tell us that E on the sixth string is the root of this chord, therefore it is an E chord of some description. The G natural on the third string (as opposed to G♯) makes this chord minor and the only other chord tone here is the B on the second string which is the fifth degree of the scale. This doesn't change the major or minor tonality of the chord. If, for example, we had a D played on the second string third fret, we would have the chord E minor seventh (Em7), because D is a minor (or flattened) seventh note in the scale of E. If we also had a G♯ instead of a G natural, we would have the chord E7.

Figure 21: Standard tuning

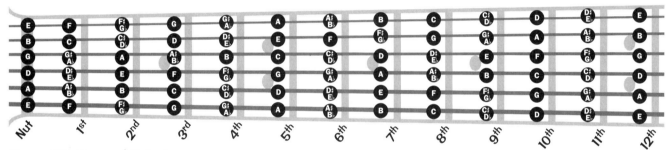

Figure 22: Dropped D tuning

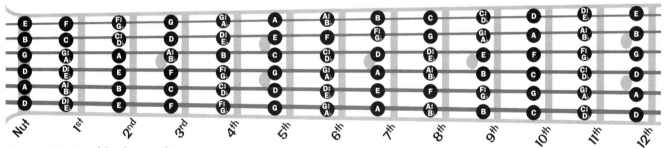

Figure 23: Double dropped D tuning

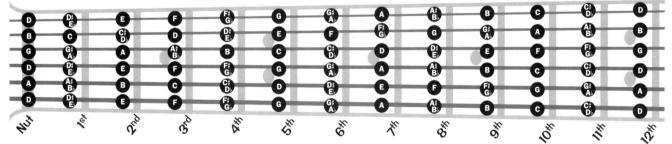

Figure 24: DADGAD tuning

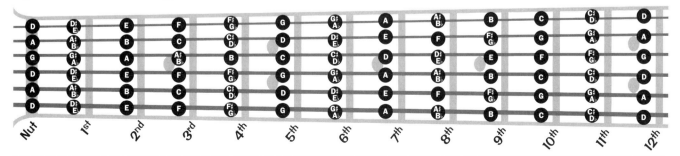

Chord inversions/voicings

Inversions (or voicings) refer to the order in which the notes of the scale appear in the chord. For example, in an E (major) chord, we have the notes E, G♯, B and E. If you play an E chord on the guitar, strumming only strings 4, 3, 2 and 1, you will hear an E chord with the notes in this order. This is called a *closed* voicing. If the notes did not appear in this order, the chord would be referred to as *semi-open* or *open* depending upon how they actually appear. Because of the nature of the guitar, we are restricted in the number of options we have to play chords in different voicings and the easiest chord shapes for different chords will mean that the voicings are different.

Modal chords & modes

The term *modal* can be a bit misleading. In its original meaning, modes refer to scales used in a melody. By this definition, every tune is modal, in that it will use predominantly, if not totally, the notes of one particular scale. The regular do-re-me scale is known as the *Ionian* mode. Modes are defined by the pattern of intervals (tone or semitone) between each note in the scale. For example, the Ionian mode has the pattern of intervals shown in **Figure 25** below.

By definition, the pattern is the same for every key. To play the Ionian mode (or scale) in any key you use this pattern of intervals to determine which notes are in the mode.

The best way to familiarise yourself with the modes is to sit at a piano and find middle C. Play a scale, starting at middle C and ending at the next C playing only the white keys. You've played the notes in the Ionian mode. If you start at the next note up, D and play *only the white keys* up to the next D, that gives you the *Dorian* mode. This has a minor sound because the third and seventh notes are flattened in relation to the Ionian mode.

The third popular mode is the *Mixolydian* mode, which you can hear if you play *only the white keys* starting at G. This mode has a major third but a flattened seventh and quite a few traditional tunes are in this mode.

The following list shows the modes in the key of C and they are found on the piano by playing the white keys starting at the notes indicated.

Dorian	D
Phrygian	E
Lydian	F
Mixolydian	G
Aeolian	A
Locrian	B

However, there is another use for the word modal which I've only heard used among folk musicians. Chords that don't have a third in them are sometimes referred to as *modal*, as the chord can be used as a minor or major. This is because the third is the note that gives the chord its major or minor tonality, so a chord without the third can be used as either a major or minor chord. For example, a D chord in DADGAD,

with just the third string fretted at the second fret does not have an F♯ (third) in it, so it falls under this definition of a modal chord.

Barré chords

A *barré* chord is one where the index finger is used like a capo. These chords can be moved up and down the fretboard since there are no open strings. The most easily adaptable chord shape for use with a barré is the E shape, followed closely by the A minor shape. In addition, many chords can be played using a partial barré. For example, if you want to play a B minor chord, you can barré the second fret on strings 1 to 5 with your index finger and finger the chord (an A minor shape) with the remaining fingers; just don't hit the sixth string!

Slash chords

Chords which have more than one title with a slash (/) between them are known as *slash chords*. This is a way of specifying the bottom-most note of the chord. For example, G/A is a G chord with an A on the bass: D/F♯ is a D chord with an F♯ on the bass, etc.

Relative minors

Every major key has its *relative minor* key. In the key of C, for example, the relative minor is A (minor). If you play the chord sequence C-Am-F-G, you will hear the relationship between C and Am clearly. The relative minor keys for the main keys used in folk music are as follows:

Key	relative minor
C	A
D	B
E	C♯
F	D
G	E
A	F♯

You will often find that in the course of the accompaniment of a tune, a chord and its relative minor are interchangeable, so relative minors are one possible option in the search for alternative chords.

Figure 25: **The Ionian mode**

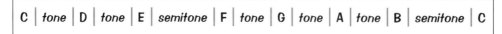

| C | tone | D | tone | E | semitone | F | tone | G | tone | A | tone | B | semitone | C |

© 2000 Dave Mallinson Publications

4·2 List of chords used in this book

Figure 26: Standard tuning chords

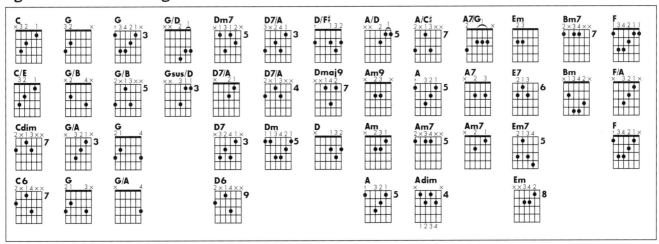

Figure 27: Dropped D chords

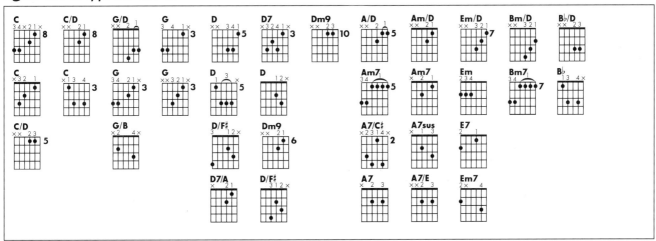

Figure 28: Double dropped D chords

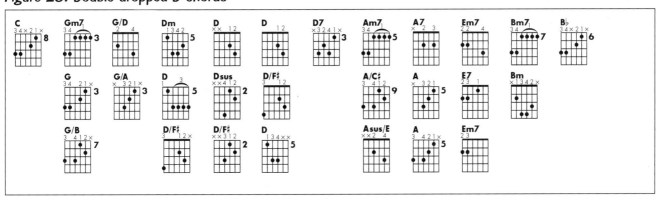

Figure 29: DADGAD chords (some names are approximate)

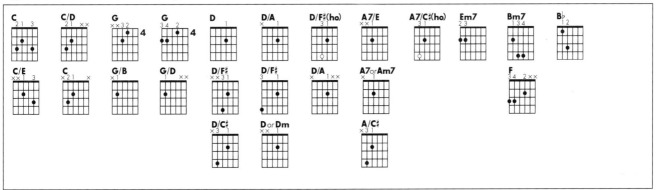

4·3 Transposition chart

You can use the following chart to determine the fret on which you need to place the capo in order to play in any particular key. For example, if you want to play in the key of D but the tune is in G, this is what you do. Find D on the top row and go down that column until you find G. Then go over to the left and you will see the capo position you need to use. With a little practice this will become second nature and you won't need the chart.

Figure 30: **Transposition chart**

Capo position	C	C♯/D♭	D	D♯/E♭	E	F	F♯/G♭	G	G♯/A♭	A	A♯/B♭	B
1	C♯/D♭	D	D♯/E♭	E	F	F♯/G♭	G	G♯/A♭	A	A♯/B♭	B	C
2	D	D♯/E♭	E	F	F♯/G♭	G	G♯/A♭	A	A♯/B♭	B	C	C♯/D♭
3	D♯/E♭	E	F	F♯/G♭	G	G♯/A♭	A	A♯/B♭	B	C	C♯/D♭	D
4	E	F	F♯/G♭	G	G♯/A♭	A	A♯/B♭	B	C	C♯/D♭	D	D♯/E♭
5	F	F♯/G♭	G	G♯/A♭	A	A♯/B♭	B	C	C♯/D♭	D	D♯/E♭	E
6	F♯/G♭	G	G♯/A♭	A	A♯/B♭	B	C	C♯/D♭	D	D♯/E♭	E	F
7	G	G♯/A♭	A	A♯/B♭	B	C	C♯/D♭	D	D♯/E♭	E	F	F♯/G♭

Mícheál Ó Domhnaill

Peerie Willie Johnson

© 2000 Dave Mallinson Publications

4·4 Running order of accompanying CD

Tracks 1 - 14 with accompaniment
Tracks 27 - 40 without accompaniment

1 Mist-covered mountain/The rakes of Kildare
2 Pigeon on the gate/The Shaskeen reel
3 The trip to Athlone/The rambling pitchfork
4 Julia Delaney/My love is in America
5 My darling asleep/Boys of the town
6 Flogging reel/The whistling postman
7 John Brady's/Hexham races
8 Pigtown fling/Roly-poly
9 Dr O'Neill/The mug of brown ale
10 Eddie Kelly's jig/Jerry's beaver hat
11 Pretty Peg/The baker
12 Fred Finn's/Music in the glen
13 Cooley's hornpipe/The home ruler
14 Shoemaker's daughter/Dinkie's reel
15 DADGAD Example 1
16 DADGAD Example 1F
17 DADGAD Example 2
18 DADGAD Example 2F
19 DADGAD Example 3
20 DADGAD Example 3F
21 DADGAD Example 4
22 DADGAD Example 4F
23 DADGAD Example 5
24 DADGAD Example 5F
25 DADGAD Example 6
26 DADGAD Example 6F
27 Mist-covered mountain/The rakes of Kildare
28 Pigeon on the gate/The Shaskeen reel
29 The trip to Athlone/The rambling pitchfork
30 Julia Delaney/My love is in America
31 My darling asleep/Boys of the town
32 Flogging reel/The whistling postman
33 John Brady's/Hexham races
34 Pigtown fling/Roly-poly
35 Dr O'Neill/The mug of brown ale
36 Eddie Kelly's jig/Jerry's beaver hat
37 Pretty Peg/The baker
38 Fred Finn's/Music in the glen
39 Cooley's hornpipe/The home ruler
40 Shoemaker's daughter/Dinkie's reel

Photo: Helen Bommarito

Randal Bays

4·5 Discography for recommended listening

Many of these artists have other albums but the listed ones have audible guitar accompaniment on almost every track. Where possible, I have listed contact information for albums that might not be available in record stores.

Randal Bays

Martin Hayes
Martin Hayes
Green Linnet GL 1127
Under The Moon
Green Linnet GL 1155
Bays and Bernstein
Pigtown Fling
Foxglove Records FG 9601
Randal Bays
Out of the Woods
Foxglove Records FG 9701
P.O. Box 30083
Seattle WA 98103
E-mail fg@teleport.com
Web
http://www.teleport.com/~fg/index.html

Ed Boyd

Red Ceil
Jump to The Sun
RCL 1 (Distributed by Gael Linn)
Flook!
Flook! Live
Smalltime Records Small 9405
Mike McGoldrick
Morning Rory
Aughrim Records Augh 01

Paul Brady

John Vesey & Paul Brady
The First Month of Summer
Shanachie
Matt Molloy, Paul Brady & Tommy Peoples
A Mighty Session
Mulligan LUN 17
Andy McGann & Paul Brady
Traditional Music of Ireland
Shanachie Shan 34011
Andy McGann, Paddy Reynolds & Paul Brady
Andy McGann, Paddy Reynolds & Paul Brady
Shanachie Shan 34008
Tommy Peoples & Paul Brady
The High Part of the Road
Shanachie Shan 34007

Dennis Cahill

Martin Hayes & Dennis Cahill
The Lonesome Touch
Green Linnet GL 1181
Live in Seattle
Green Linnet GL 1195

Ian Carr

Ian Carr & Karen Tweed
SHHH!
BMG-Ariola/ARIS 876 928
Fyace
Fyac 001
Swäp
Swäp
AM 735
Kathryn Tickell
Common Ground
CRO 220
The Kathryn Tickell Band
CRO 227
The Gathering
PRK 39

Steve Cooney

Begley & Cooney
Meitheal
Hummingbird HB 0004
Martin Hayes
Under The Moon
Green Linnet GL 1155
Sean Smyth
The Blue Fiddle
Mulligan LUN 060
Vinnie Kilduff
The Boys from Blue Hill
Mulligan LUN 050
Sharon Shannon
Sharon Shannon
ROCDG 8
Each Little Thing
GRA 0226
Alan Kelly
Out of The Blue
Blackbox BMM 001
Johnny Connolly
Drioball na Fainleoige
CI 127
Dermot Byrne
Dermot Byrne
Hummingbird HB 0007

John Doyle

Solas
Solas
Shanachie Shan 78002
Sunny Spells and Scattered Showers
Shanachie Shan 78010
The Words That Remain
Shanachie Shan 78023
Eileen Ivers
Wild Blue
Green Linnet GL 1166
Joannie Madden
Song of the Irish Whistle
Hearts of Space HS 11060

Donogh Hennessey

Sharon Shannon
Out the Gap
ROCDG 8
Each Little Thing
GRA 0226
Lunasa
Lunasa
LSA 001
Alan Kelly
Out of The Blue
Blackbox BMM 001
Brendan Larrissey
A Flick of the Wrist
Cross Border Media CBM 016
Donogh Hennessey & Mark Crickard
The Hurricane

Mark Kelly

Donncha Ó Briain
Donncha Ó Briain
Gael Linn CEF 083
Charlie Lennon & Mick O'Connor
Lucky in Love
Comhaltas CL 22
Máire Bhreathnach
Angel's Candles
Starc S 593
Altan
Altan
Green Linnet GL 1078
Horse with a Heart
Green Linnet GL 1095
The Red Crow
Green Linnet GL 1109
Harvest Storm
Green Linnet GL 1117
The First Ten Years
Green Linnet GL 1153
Island Angel
Green Linnet GL 1137
Blackwater
Virgin V 2796
Runaway Sunday
Virgin V 2836

Arty McGlynn

Frankie Gavin, Aiden Coffey & Arty McGlynn
Irlande
Oscora C 560021
Arty McGlynn
McGlynn's Fancy
Emerald BER 011 or LD 19351
Nollaig Casey & Arty McGlynn
Causeway
Tara 3035
Lead The Knave
MCG 1
Port an Phiobaire
Paddy Keenan
Gael Linn CEF 099
Four Men & A Dog
Barking Mad
Cross Border Media CBM 001
Shifting Gravel
Special Delivery SPD1047
Seamus McGuire & John Lee
The Missing Reel
Gael Linn CEF 146
Matt Molloy
The Stony Steps
Claddagh CCF 18
Music from Matt Molloy's
Real World 26
Shadows on Stone
Virgin VE 930
Sean Keane & Matt Molloy
Contentment is Wealth
Green Linnet GL 1058
Liam O'Flynn
The Piper
Tara 3037
Out to an Other Side
Tara 3031
The Given Note
Tara 3034
The Piper's Call
Tara 3037
Sean Keane, Matt Malloy & Liam O'Flynn
The Fire Aflame
Claddagh CCF 30
Patrick Street
Patrick Street
Green Linnet GL 1071

Patrick Street II
Green Linnet GL 1088
Irish Times
Green Linnet GL 1033
All in Good TIme
Green Linnet GL 1125
De Dannan
Half Set in Harlem
Green Linnet GL 1113
Donal Lunny
Donal Lunny
Gael Linn CEF 133
Beginish
Beginish
Inis 001

Mícheál Ó Domhnaill

Bothy Band
Bothy Band 1975
Green Linnet GL 3011
Old Hag You Have Killed Me
Green Linnet GL 3005
Out of the wind into the sun
Green Linnet GL 3013
Afterhours
Green Linnet GL 3016
Relativity
Cunninghams and Ó Domhnaills
Green Linnet GL 1059
Gathering Pace
Green Linnet GL 1076
Mícheál Ó Domhnaill & Kevin Burke
Promenade
Mulligan LUN 028
Portland
Green Linnet GL 1041

Dáithí Sproule

Skara Brae
Skara Brae
Gael Linn CEF031
James Kelly, Paddy O'Brien & Dáithí Sproule
Is It Yourself?
Shanachie Shan 29015
Spring in the Air
Shanachie Shan 29018
Traditional Music of Ireland
Shanachie Shan 34014
James Kelly
Capel Street
Bow Hand Records
Tommy Peoples
The Iron Man
Shanachie Shan 79044
Seamus & Manus Maguire
Carousel
Gael Linn CEF 105
Liz Carroll
Liz Carroll
Green Linnet GL 1902
Paddy O'Brien
Stranger at the Gate
Green Linnet GL 1091
Trian
Trian
Flying Fish FF 70586
Trian II
Green Linnet GL 1159
Liz Carroll & Peter Ostroushko
A Heart Made of Glass
Green Linnet GL 1123
Altan
Blackwater
Virgin V 2796
Island Angel
Green Linnet GL 1137
Runaway Sunday
Virgin V 2836

© 2000 Dave Mallinson Publications